MYTHS OF THE WORLD

TALES OF NATIVE AMERICA

MYTHS OF THE WORLD

TALES OF NATIVE AMERICA

EDWARD W. HUFFSTETLER

MetroBooks

MetroBooks

AN IMPRINT OF FRIEDMAN/FAIRFAX PUBLISHERS

©1996 by Michael Friedman Publishing Group, Inc.

Library of Congress Cataloging-in-Publication data available upon request.

Editor: Sharyn Rosart
Art Director: Jeff Batzli
Designer: Susan E. Livingston
Photography Editor: Colleen A. Branigan

Color separations by HBM Print Pte. Ltd.
Printed in China by Leefung-Asco Printers Ltd.

For bulk purchases and special sales, please contact:
Friedman/Fairfax Publishers
Attention: Sales Department
15 West 26th Street
New York, NY 10010
212/685-6610 FAX 212/685-1307

PHOTOGRAPHY CREDITS

Archive Photos: 2, 34 (left), 54 (left), 55, 69, 76–77, 80 (bottom), 82, 87, 92, 105; ©American Stock: 84; ©Hirz: 88–89; ©Lambert: 100–101

American Museum of Natural History: 70, 79, 81 (top), 99; P. Hollembeak/O. Bauer: 50; C. Chesek: 94; Don Eiler: 102 (top); Courtesy Department of Library Services: Neg# 243090 (copied), Scott: 62; Neg# 242615 (copied), J. Kirschner, 1921: 63; Neg.#15985: 14–15; Rodman Wanamaker, Neg.# 316473: 74, Neg.# 316740: 91

© Edward S. Curtis/Courtesy Museum of New Mexico, Neg# 65118: 18

© D. DeHarport/Peabody Museum, Harvard University: 35

Field Museum of Natural History, Chicago: Neg.# A15907: 72; Neg.# A15356: 96

FPG: 10, 34 (right), 57; ©Dave Bartruff: 13 (bottom); ©Jeffry Myers: 20; ©Ingvard Eide: 21; ©Lee Foster: 22; ©Frank Fiske: 41; ©Willard Clay: 43; ©Herb and Dorothy McLaughlin: 90

Library of Congress: 48

National Museum of American Art/Art Resource: Sharp, Joseph Henry. *Sunset Dance-Ceremony to the Sun*: 27; Catlin, George. *Blue Medicine*: 44, *View on the Wisconsin River*: 78, *Little Bear*: 98

National Museum of the American Indian/Smithsonian Institution: 29, 58, 60, 61, 65 (top), 66 (both), 80 (top), 81 (bottom), 97

©1994 North Wind Pictures: 13 (top), 46, 56 (bottom) 64, 65, 103

H. Armstrong Roberts: © Camerique/Fotopic: 11; © C.P. Cushing Collection: 32, 36; © Camerique: 40

©The Rockwell Museum, Corning, New York: Stanley, John Mix. *The Smoke Signal*: 42

Schoharie Museum of the Iroquois Indian: 24, 54 (right)

Tom Stack & Associates: ©Lorran Meares: 8; ©John Shaw: 51; ©Gerald & Buff Corsi: 73; ©Rod Planck: 85; ©R.C. Simpson: 93

Tony Stone Images: ©Art Wolfe: 56 (top); ©Bruce Hands: 47

© Superstock: 28, 31 (top); Whiteside, Frank Reed. *Corn Dance*. David Gallery, Philadelphia: 33 (top)

© Stephen Trimble: 6, 16 (top), 17, 25, 86, 104, 106–107, 108, 109; Original artwork by Lillian Salvador: 30; Original artwork by Rose Chino Garcia/Courtesy School of American Research: 33 (bottom); Courtesy Cameron Trading Post: 68

©UPI/Bettmann: 12, 16 (bottom), 38–39

©Werner Forman Archive/Art Resource: Haffenreffer Museum of Anthropology, Brown University, RI: 19; Maxwell Museum of Anthropology, Albuquerque: 26; Royal Ontario Museum, Toronto, Canada: 52; Provincial Museum, Victoria, British Columbia, Canada: 102 (bottom)

The Wildlife Collection: ©John Guistina: 31 (bottom); ©D. Robert Franz: 53

Wyoming State Museum: 67

DEDICATION

To Susan, Rebecca, John, and Hannah for all their love and support.

ACKNOWLEDGMENTS

I would like to thank Mr. Lance Kenney for his word processing
efficiency, Ms. Doris Wampler for the loan of her many resources,
Mr. Terrance Barkley for his help and encouragement, and
the staff at the Bridgewater College library for all their assistance.

CONTENTS

MYTH AND THE
NATIVE AMERICAN
VIEW OF THE WORLD

Those of us who live in the urbanized modern world, and whose cultural background is primarily European, often have difficulty coming to grips with the myths, stories, and legends of other, more anciently rooted cultures. We may feel embarrassed, as though we have been caught eavesdropping on a private conversation. Or we may be confused by the fact that we are unable to identify those elements of narrative structure we have come to expect in a story: the "once upon a time" opening, the rising action involving a

To the natives of North America, the landscape is literally alive, with the same consciousness as the people and animals that occupy it. In fact, landscape, such as this southwestern scene from Chaco Culture National Historic Park in New Mexico, plays so vital a role in Native American mythology that it often functions as a character itself within the tales.

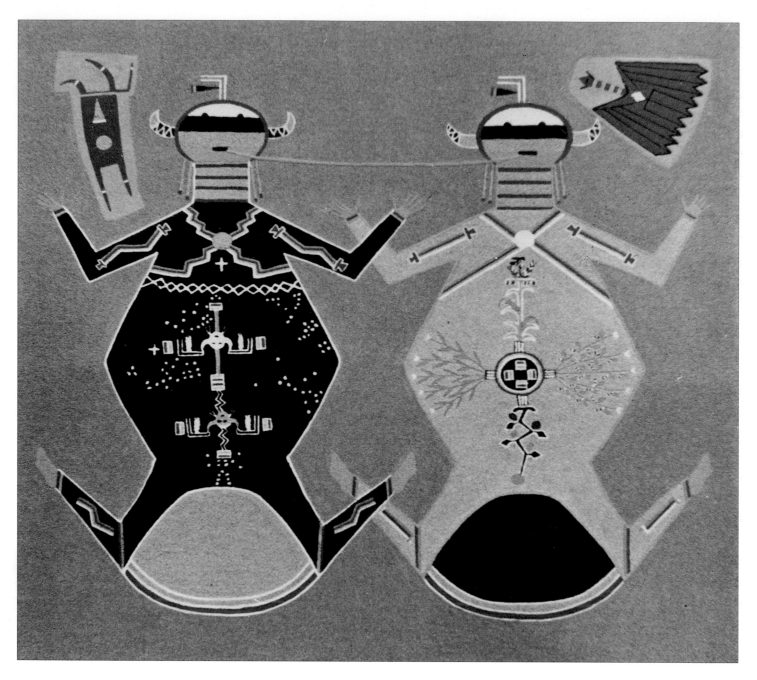

Different cultures celebrate their myths in different ways. For Navajo sandpainters, artistic displays of mythic figures, such as Father Sky and Mother Earth depicted here, become sacred expressions of their time-honored stories.

conflict, the dramatic climax, the resolution, and, of course, the moral at the end. The stories seem to have a plot, yes, but often they do not include the pattern of action we have come to recognize or expect. At the end of the story, we may feel that we've missed the point entirely.

Native American stories, especially, present the uninitiated reader with these kinds of quandaries. Add to this the rather exotic nature of some of the stories, their predominantly cyclical and serial structure, and the cultural knowledge one must possess to un-

derstand certain elements within each cycle, and the frustrations grow. Before presenting a representative sampling of Native American myths, this book will provide an introduction to the cultural context in which the stories evolved and have been told for centuries. In this way the myths will become more intelligible to the non-Indian reader so that even the most enigmatic tales can be understood and appreciated.

On the surface there are certain clearly defined differences between Native American stories and those that originated in Europe.

First, the stories may have a variety of characters, not all of whom seem related to the narrative. Indeed, characters are sometimes purposely divided so that several characters function as different aspects of the same character type. This process, referred to as "splitting" or "decomposing" by noted author and collector of Indian tales John Bierhorst, can produce a rather striking narrative effect. Another surface difference of the stories is their tendency to build one upon another, a sort of layering effect that provides a deeper, richer level of meaning for any given story as it is told year after year. In fact many Native American stories consist of a string of smaller tales, a series or cycle of stories, that together form a single complex, layered saga.

Although the novice reader may not readily identify this layering quality or even know that there are other stories in the cycle, it is still apparent from the beginning that certain characters, such as the Trickster, or certain narrative elements, such as descriptions of landscape, have a more symbolic, resonant presence than one might expect in a single tale. In fact these elements tend to function, for the most part, the way literary symbols function in modern fiction and drama, giving the entire work a deeper, more profound level of meaning.

Yet the reader who looks for symbolism beyond these resonant elements, the sort of symbolism we have become accustomed to in the European literary tradition, will often be disappointed. In Native American stories, one rarely finds the sort of metaphors, poetic comparisons, or intentional juxtapositions of objects and descriptions from which we have learned to draw an array of moral conclusions; even in our simple fairy tales, there are easily recognizable moral comparisons—for example, good guys wear white, bad guys wear black, evil beings are physically ugly, physically strong characters are often less intelli-

gent, and so on. Native American stories lack this symbolic code, and one should not assume in any case that the symbolic lexicon of Indian tales would be familiar to the non-Indian reader. Native American stories as a whole often function as extended metaphors, providing sweeping comparisons about human nature and its relationship to the natural or spiritual world.

These superficial differences aside, there is another, more profound difference that ex-

Like all authentic art, Native American stories resonate with the fluid vitality of the cultures themselves and bring together all other native art forms including dance, costuming, music, and the visual arts.

ists between Native American stories and our own literary traditions. In the European tradition, literature has become primarily entertainment, that is, entertainment that occasionally teaches a moral lesson or illustrates a moral or historic truth. But for Native Americans, myths, legends, and stories do much more. Each individual story provides a glimpse of a much larger picture, a piece of a mosaic of thought that encompasses every aspect of the varied and different Native American cultures. In short, these stories reveal a people for whom storytelling is the equivalent of all we in the industrialized West achieve in science, religion, medicine, philosophy, and the arts. Stories act as both the repository of knowledge and as the building blocks of the structures upon which all knowledge depends. The stories do not simply reflect the Native American view of the world; they embody it. We readily understand how myths can explain and order the world; we can empathize with creation stories, legends of cultural heroes, and so on. But where Native American myths go further is in the underlying belief that all life is directed and

shaped by these stories. As long as the people have their stories intact, they have an identifiable cultural power, which enables them to withstand and survive anything that might befall them. Consequently the storytellers themselves, especially those who are more experienced, have immense prestige within

ABOVE: The Kiowa legend of the arrow-maker serves to illustrate the importance of stories to a culture for whom stories reposited all their collective knowledge and all the various means by which they related to a hostile world.

LEFT: A Kiowa warrior dances during the celebratory ritual of the Red Earth Festival.

OPPOSITE: Many famous Native American leaders were also gifted storytellers. Chief Santanta of the Kiowa was known for his ability to interpret stories and make them applicable to immediate situations the Kiowa faced, using traditional stories to help devise battle strategies and make plans for the future, consulting the ancient wisdom of his ancestors.

their respective cultures. They not only shape the plot and the direction of the narratives that provide their people with a coherent understanding of who and what they are, but they also serve a quasi-religious function by interpreting new events and ideas, synthesizing them into narratives that convey essential spiritual truths.

N. Scott Momaday, a noted Native American author and scholar (and a Kiowa Indian from western Oklahoma), often uses the Kiowa legend of the arrow maker to illustrate the power that storytelling has in his culture. The Kiowa were a southern plains tribe of nomadic buffalo hunters and warriors. Their most celebrated leader was Santanta, whose skills at horseback riding and storytelling were equally well known among plains tribes. The story of the arrow maker begins with a description of how the Kiowa make arrows by straightening them with their teeth, then drawing them in their bow to check if they are straight. Once the procedure is explained, the story itself begins.

Once there was a man and his wife who were alone at night in their tepee. By the light of the fire, the man was making arrows. While making these arrows, the man suddenly caught sight of something through a slit in the seam of the tepee wall. Someone was outside looking in. The man said to his wife, "Someone is outside looking in, but do not be afraid. Let's speak casually, as of ordinary things." He then took up an arrow and straightened it with his teeth. Then, following the usual process, he put the arrow to the bow to check it. He took aim, first in this direction, then in that direction, and all the while he was talking, as if to his wife. "I know that you are out there. If you are Kiowa, then you will know what I'm saying, and you will speak your name." But there was no answer, and the man went on in the same way, pointing the arrow all around. At last his aim fell

Myths concerning the afterlife varied from culture to culture because concepts surrounding death varied, ranging from no concept of an afterlife at all to elaborate visions of "the other side." Pictured here is a plains burial ground.

ABOVE: Pictographs, such as this one from the Zuni Village of the Great Kivas, display mythical figures and legendary heroes.

RIGHT: Credited with beginning a new Renaissance in Native American studies, the Kiowa author N. Scott Momaday, through works such as *The Way to Rainy Mountain* and *House Made of Dawn*, has brought Native American myths and stories to a much wider audience.

upon the place where his enemy stood, and he let go of the string. The arrow went straight to the enemy's heart and killed him.

Momaday uses this story to illustrate the importance of language and storytelling to his people. Like the arrow maker, much of their existence depends on a rather tenuous connection between language and action. The arrow maker in the story has really only one weapon and that is language. He uses language to probe the unknown, and by so doing he gains an advantage over external things that would do him harm. In much the same way, Native Americans' stories function to explain and give shape to the unknowns around them; the stories give the Indians their identity and define for them those external things of which they are unsure. By telling stories and then testing them through experience, the people gain a kind of knowl-

edge, a unique type of advantage over events and over the natural world that they otherwise wouldn't have.

On one level Native American stories almost always illustrate the power and the dangers inherent in nature, while maintaining a reverence for that power. The myths help explain, in a sense, what nature is up to or man's proper response to nature. Often myths are directly tied to particular landscapes and thereby identify not only a people but a place as well, connecting a given people spiritually to a particular place. This element of landscape is often so important that there seems to be a separate spiritual message to the listeners, as though, aside from the story itself, the storyteller is also implicitly saying, "Yes, I'm telling you a story that has a moral point to make, but beyond that, if you are to be a member of this tribe, you must know also that

this place is sacred to us and how that came about." Likewise there will be many regional variations of any widespread Native American story that highlight the particular sacred lands of that tribe, and often this detail of landscape will be the only essential element of the story to change from tribe to tribe. For instance those along the northwest coast and around the Great Lakes often tell of giant sea monsters and lake men who live beneath the water; for them water was mysterious and sacred. In the southwest, many similar legends develop around corn and corn production—complete with monsters or supernatural beings—because for these tribes the agricultural process was a life-giving, sacred mystery. Despite these details, the stories themselves have striking similarities.

There are even more universal elements within the stories, characters, and plots told

Pictographic representation of myths dates back thousands of years, creating stark images, such as this Zuni figure, of the power of Native storytellers.

All rituals, such as
the Cheyenne Sun
Dance Ceremony these
warriors have pledged
to participate in,
begin with an ancient
legend about their
origins. Usually the
teacher-god who
instructs the people
in the details of the
ritual is a young
woman or a child,
since most cultures
believed that women
and children have
a more direct
connection to the
sacred energy of life.

repeatedly by most Native American cultures, such as characters like primordial giants or giant animals, legends of godlike twins, and Trickster stories—elements that transcend the physical landscape or particular tribal custom. We share many of these universal elements with Native Americans in our own literary traditions. Anthropomorphic stories (featuring animals personified with human characteristics) and stories of ghosts and descriptions of the hereafter are examples of this more universal narrative type.

Along with their understanding of the power and responsibility of their role, Native American storytellers are keenly attuned to their specific audiences, and often make an effort to tailor their stories to suit their listeners. Stories are frequently told to children, a fact that may surprise us given that many of these tales are full of frankly scatological and sexual references, both in terms of language and behavior. Early ethnographers and missionaries typically were appalled to hear Trickster stories being told to giggling children who would shriek with laughter and cover their mouths in embarrassment at the more outrageous sections. But the myths as a whole are far more than children's stories, and every gathering of the people invariably includes time for telling stories, appropriate for the occasion and season, or appropriate in a more emotional sense. Stories told among adults are meant to accomplish a variety of tasks, including the easing of emotional pain,

Often rituals, or the legends that explain their origins, were depicted on buffalo hides, sometimes in order to commemorate a particular ritual event or perhaps to be used by shamans as a future reference. This Lakota hide painting illustrates a Sun Dance performed during the 1880s.

OPPOSITE: Gifted storytellers were cherished by their people. This plains Indian elder would gather an audience and begin with a traditional phrase such as: "A long time ago it was the same even as it is now," or, perhaps, "Let me offer you a story about that."

and there are stories for all emotional and psychological conditions. Stories for those who are grieving, for example, are common. And, of course, stories always teach a lesson on some level, be it psychological or practical.

Bierhorst identifies four primary types of Native American myth. The first type explains the world—how it came about, what its purpose is, and so on. The second type depicts various kinds of family drama, reflecting the different social and familial structures and their functions in the society. The third category of myth explores the concepts of good and evil, explaining the values of the society and the process by which it distinguishes right and wrong. The fourth type of myth examines the concept of crossing a threshold, such as the threshold between childhood and adulthood or that between life and death, this world and the next.

For our purposes the tales have been categorized in an even more basic way. The first group includes creation stories, that is, stories involving the creation of the physical earth. Next come stories of cultural origins, explaining how societies were formed and how their customs and rituals began. After that are stories of animals, a category that Native American cultures share with European literary traditions. Next come stories of heroes and warriors, a category that shows surprising variation among different regions. Then come the Trickster tales, followed by stories of love and lust, and finally ghost stories and stories of death and the hereafter. Naturally these categories are somewhat arbitrary. In fact it may seem that some stories do not fit well within their assigned category or that others could fit well in at least two categories. Still, the groupings should help the beginning reader of Native American tales identify the common elements and the range of stories that make up what we collectively refer to as Native American mythology.

HOW THE EARTH BEGAN: STORIES OF PHYSICAL CREATION

Stories of the creation of the physical world are remarkably similar across Native American cultures. With the exception of those from the southwest and arctic regions, most Indian creation tales share the same basic elements: a watery world with no land; the fashioning of land from mud, usually brought up by aquatic animals or heroes; powerful twin gods who frequently represent good and evil; and the ambiguity of good and evil in the natural world. Many also include a struggle between primeval monsters.

For most Native American tribes, the earth began slowly, small bit by small bit, much the same way the Hopi create their basketry, each swirl slowly expanding from a single origin, eventually creating a complex and beautiful design.

The legend of Turtle Island, the most common story of physical creation, is truly a pan-Indian myth, specific to no single culture but believed by many. According to the legend, small creatures created the earth by bringing handfuls of mud up from the bottom of a primordial sea and placing them on the back of a giant turtle.

The story of Turtle Island, sometimes called "the legend of the turtle continent," is a good example of a Native American creation story, not only because it has many of the elements just named, but also because it is truly pan-Indian, belonging to no particular tribe but known by most. Almost all the eastern and plains Indian tribes have some variation of the Turtle Island story, even though they may also have more complex creation stories that are particular to their cultures.

The story goes that in the beginning there was nothing but water. All the animals had to swim continuously without rest. Finally some animals got together and decided to do something to create a home. Muskrat, beaver, mink, otter, water beetle, or toad (depending on the particular tribal affiliation of the storyteller) decided to dive down to the bottom of the water and scoop up a handful of mud. Returning to the surface, he patted the mud onto the back of an enormous turtle, then dove for more. Others joined in, diving down and bringing back mud for the turtle's back. Eventually, as the mud dried, land was formed, and the animals had a home. Now we all ride together on the back of a giant turtle covered in mud.

The story is simple but instructive in terms of how to read a Native American creation story. The emphasis is not on the creation per se and not on a scientific explanation for the earth's development, but rather on the actions necessary to create it. In this story the point is that the animals could not escape their situation as long as they each thought only of themselves. Cooperation was necessary to form the land, and cooperation is necessary, the native storyteller would argue, to maintain it.

It is just this sort of contextual emphasis that makes creation stories so interesting but often difficult to interpret. Another element of many creation stories is the presence of twin gods, one good and one evil. Clearly the implication is that nature can be either good and benevolent or evil and cruel. Nature includes both elements and hence is often created by the two opposite, yet related, forces.

In the southwest region, creation myths commonly include the idea that there are four or five worlds layered, one on top of another, and that people emerged from the lower worlds to the upper ones by climbing a reed or stalk through an opening in the sky. (Curiously, the northwest creation legends often portray a cultural hero descending, rather than ascending, from a hole in the sky to the world below.) Anthropologists speculate that subconsciously this type of story may be a rudimentary metaphor for evolution, a recognition that we have ascended from some other state to a higher one or that we have fallen since some "golden age" when we were

According to the pictographs displayed on the rockface, this site on Sprit Mountain in Nevada, near Lake Mead, is the place of emergence for the Yuma tribe, the account of which they have told for centuries.

in a more perfect state; both ideas are common in the European philosophical and religious traditions.

All speculations aside, creation stories are uncannily parallel across North America. For example, some variation of the story of the Good Creator and His Evil Twin is told among many native peoples, and it illustrates several elements discussed above. This partial version of a lengthy cycle of tales is taken from several sources, including Natalie Curtis' "Creation Myths of the Cochans (Yuma Indians)" published in *The Craftsman 16* (1909). The story comes from the Yuma people, a small tribe that inhabited a region straddling southeastern California and southwestern Arizona.

Native stories were often expressed as art and used more directly in ceremonies. This Pueblo pottery bowl, depicting the mythic figures of good and evil, would be buried with the dead and punctured to release the dead person's spirit.

THE GOOD CREATOR AND HIS EVIL TWIN

[YUMA]

This is how the world started. First there was only water. Then out of the water rose a steamy, cloudy mist, and it became the sky. Deep down in the water lived the Creator, but he was without form and did not move, and he was two creatures at that time—twins.

Then the waters stirred and gushed and clamored, and out of the spray and foam rose the first twin, the good twin. With closed eyes he pushed back the waves and came to the surface. He stood on top of the water, opened his eyes, and saw the universe for the first time. Then he named himself Kokomaht, which means "All-Father."

And from the depths of the water, a voice called out to Kokomaht, "My brother, how did you come up? With your eyes open or with your eyes closed?"

This voice belonged to the evil twin, and Kokomaht wanted to make it more difficult for him to do evil things in the universe. So Kokomaht lied to him, saying, "I opened my eyes while I was underwater." The second twin opened his eyes as he came up, and when he reached the surface, he couldn't see. He was blind from that time on. Kokomaht said, "I name you Bakotahl—the Blind One."

"Now," Kokomaht said, "I shall make the earth."

Kokomaht stirred the water into a foaming whirlpool with his hand. It gushed and swelled and bubbled, and when it subsided, there was land. Then Kokomaht sat down upon it.

Bakotahl was angry because he would have liked to create the earth, but he said nothing and settled down by Kokomaht's side. The Blind Evil One said to himself, "I shall make something with a head, with arms and legs. I can make it out of the earth." Bakotahl formed something resembling a human being, but it wasn't right. Instead of hands and feet there were lumps. It had neither fingers nor toes. Bakotahl was ashamed and hid it from Kokomaht.

Then Kokomaht said, "I feel like making something." Out of mud he shaped a being that was perfect in every way. It had hands and feet, fingers and toes, even fingernails and toenails. Kokomaht waved this being four times toward the north and then stood it on its feet. It moved, it walked, it was alive. It was a man. Kokomaht made another being in the same way, and it was alive. It was a woman.

Bakotahl went on trying to make humans, piecing together seven beings out of the earth at his feet. None of them was right. "What are you making?" Kokomaht asked.

"People," answered Bakotahl.

"Here," said Kokomaht, "feel these people I've made. Yours have no hands or feet. Here, feel, mine have fingers, thumbs, to work, to fashion things, to draw bows, to pick fruit." Kokomaht examined the beings Bakotahl had formed. "These are no good," he said, and threw them in the water. Bakotahl was so enraged that he dove down deep beneath the water, which made it gush and rumble. From the depths he sent up the whirlwind, bringer

For most Native American peoples, the world was made up of opposing forces, good against evil, light against darkness, truth against falsehood. It was a balance of these forces that kept the world stable, and it was this balance that all warriors tried to maintain.

of all evil. Kokomaht stepped on the whirlwind and stopped it—except for a little whiff that slipped out from under his foot. In that whiff were contained all the sicknesses that plague people to this day.

"You must learn how to increase," said Kokomaht to the people he had made. To teach them, he begat a son. Out of nothing, without any help from a woman, he gave

birth to him and named him Komashtam'ho. He told men and women not to live apart but to join together and rear children.

Still something was missing. "It is too dark," said Kokomaht. "There should be some light." So he made the moon, the morning star, and all the other stars. Then he said, "My work is done. Whatever I have not finished, my son Komashtam'ho will finish." With that

Kokomaht lay down on the earth and Hanyi, the Frog, who was buried under the earth, sucked the breath from his body and he died.

After a time, Komashtam'ho said, "I will begin to make what my father could not finish." He spat into his hand and from his spittle made a disk. He took it and threw it up into the sky toward the east. It began to shine. "This is the sun," Komashtam'ho told the people. "Watch it move toward the west, watch it light up the universe."

Then Komashtam'ho chose one man, Marhokuvek, to help him put the world in order. The first thing that Marhokuvek did was to say, "Now, you people, as a sign that you mourn the death of your father Kokomaht, you should cut your hair short." Then all the people, animals, and birds did as they had been told. The animals at this time were people also. They looked like humans. But when he saw them Komashtam'ho said, "These animals and birds don't look well with their hair cut," and changed them into coyotes and deer, wild turkeys, and roadrunners—into the animals and birds we have now.

After some time, Komashtam'ho let fall a great rain, the kind that never stops. There was a flood in which many of the animals were drowned. Marhokuvek was greatly alarmed. "Komashtam'ho, what are you doing?" he cried.

"Some of these animals are too wild. Some have big teeth and claws and are dangerous. Also there are far too many of them. So I am killing them off with this flood."

"No, Komashtam'ho, please stop the flood," pleaded Marhokuvek. "The people need many of these animals for food. They like to hear the songs of the birds. Rain and flood make the world too cold, and the people can't stand it."

So Komashtam'ho made a big fire to cause the waters to evaporate. The fire was so hot and fierce that even Komashtam'ho himself was slightly burned. Ever since that time, the deserts around here have been hot, and the people are used to the great heat.

Komashtam'ho then took a huge pole and smashed the house of his dead father, which afterward became the custom among the Yuma, and rooted up the ground on which it had stood. Water welling up from the run made by the pole became the Colorado River. And in it swam the beings that Bakotahl—the Blind Evil One—had formed, the creatures without hands or feet, toes or fingers. These were the fish and other water animals.

Now Bakotahl, the Blind Evil One, is still under the earth and does bad things. Usually he lies down there quietly, but sometimes he turns over. Then there is a great noise of thunder, the earth trembles and splits open, and mountains crack, while flames and smoke shoot out of their summits. Then the people are afraid and say, "The Blind Evil One is stirring down below."

Everything that is good comes from Kokomaht and his son Komashtam'ho, and everything evil comes from Bakotahl. This is still the way things are.

•

Another variation of the typical creation story can be found among the Cherokee, a southeastern tribe who lived in the southern Appalachian mountains in what is now the Carolinas, Georgia, and Tennessee. This creation tale features mostly animal characters, with one exception—the supreme being they call Someone Powerful. This story appears in an array of sources,

Steeped in tradition and an elaborate web of stories, all Yuma artifacts bear the stamp of ancient tales. This cradleboard, decorated with feathers and other insignia, was designed to protect and calm the infant inside.

including one version told at a Cherokee treaty council meeting in New York City in 1975 and recorded by Richard Erdoes in *American Indian Myths and Legends* (1984).

HOW THE EARTH WAS MADE

[CHEROKEE]

This ceramic pot from Acoma Pueblo in New Mexico is decorated with mythic animal figures, each one representing a tale in a specific cycle of tales.

In the beginning, there was nothing but water. Living creatures existed, however, but they lived high up, above the rainbow, and it was crowded up there. "We are all squished together," the animals said. "We need more room." Wondering what was under the water, they sent Water Beetle to take a look around.

Water Beetle skimmed over the surface but couldn't find any solid footing, so he dived down to the bottom and brought up a little dab of soft, watery mud. Magically, the mud spread out in the four directions and became this huge island we are living on, this earth. Someone Powerful then fastened it to the sky ceiling with leather cords and thongs.

At first the earth was flat, soft, and wet. All the animals were eager to live on it, and they kept sending down birds to see if the mud had dried and hardened enough that they could live on it. But the birds all flew back and said that there was still no spot they could perch on yet.

Then the animals sent Grandfather Buzzard down. He flew very close and saw that the earth was still soft, but when he glided low over what would become Cherokee country, he found that the mud was getting harder. By that time Buzzard was tired and dragging. When he flapped his wings down, they made a valley where they touched the earth; when he swept them up, they made a mountain. The animals watching from above the rainbow said, "If he keeps on, there will be only mountains," and they made him come back. That's why we have so many mountains in Cherokee country today.

At last the earth was hard and dry enough for the animals to live on, and the animals came down from the sky. They couldn't see very well because they had no sun or moon, and someone said, "Let's grab Sun from up there behind the rainbow! Let's get him down here with us too!" They pulled Sun down and they told him, "Here's a path for you," and showed him the way to go—from east to west.

Now they had light, but it was much too hot, because Sun was too close to the earth. The crawfish had his back sticking out of a stream, and Sun burned it red. His meat was spoiled forever, and the people still won't eat crawfish.

Everyone asked the holy men, the shamans, to please put Sun higher. They pushed him up as high as a man, but it was still too hot. So they pushed him farther, but it wasn't far enough. They tried four times, and when they had Sun up to the height of four men, he was just hot enough. Everyone was happy then, so they left him there.

Before making humans, Someone Powerful had created plants and animals and had told them to stay awake and watch for seven days and seven nights. (This is just what young men do today when they fast and prepare for a ceremony.) But most of the plants

and animals couldn't manage it. Some fell asleep after one day, some after two days, some after three. Among the animals, only the owl and the mountain lion were still awake after seven days and nights. That's why they were given the gift of seeing in the dark so that they can hunt at night.

Among the trees and other plants, only the cedar, pine, holly, and laurel were still awake on the eighth morning. Someone Powerful said to them, "Because you watched and kept awake as you had been told, you will not lose your hair in the winter." So these plants stay green all year long.

After creating plants and animals, Someone Powerful made a man and his sister. The man poked his sister with a fish and told her to give birth. After seven days she had a baby, and after seven more days she had another, and every seven days yet another came. The humans increased so quickly that Someone Powerful, thinking there would soon be no

ABOVE: Cherokee medicine men, such as this shaman from Tsa-la-gi Village in Oklahoma, were the guardians of the people's legends and were charged with the continuity of the ancient stories.

LEFT: Owls were almost universally symbolic among native peoples, representing everything from death itself to the wisdom all great hunters share—cunning, tenacity, and strength. At other times, owls were more comical, representing impatience and intolerance.

more room on this earth, arranged things so that a woman could have only one child every year. And that's how it still is today.

•

This more traditional southwestern tribal myth of creation comes from the Pueblo people who live in the Acoma township outside Albuquerque, New Mexico, and it has been recorded in several sources, including a version by Daryll Forde in *Folk-lore* (vol. 41, 1930). As a typical southwestern tale, this layered cycle of stories, the main portion of which is recorded here, features the ascent from a lower world to a higher one.

This nineteenth-century Hopi man is descending into Antelope kiva to participate in a ritual at the Walpi Pueblo. The patterns of paint on his upper body are the result of his vision and follow a traditional mythic design.

CLIMBING TO THE UPPER WORLD

[ACOMA PUEBLO]

In the beginning two female human beings were formed. There was land already, but no one knows how long it had been around. The two girls had no light, but as they grew up they became aware of each other through their sense of touch.

When they had reached maturity, a spirit, Tsitctinako, spoke to them and cared for them. Slowly they began to think and act for themselves. One day they asked the spirit to appear to them. But Tsitctinako replied only that it was not allowed to meet them.

The women asked the spirit why they had to live in the dark without knowing each other by name. It told them that they were under the earth (called *nuk'timi*) and that they must be patient until everything was ready for them to go up into the light. During the long time that they waited, Tsitctinako taught them their language.

Tsitctinako then said, "Here are baskets with many useful things. Inside you have the seeds of four types of trees. Plant them. You will use the trees to climb up." Because the sisters could not see, they felt each object in their baskets and asked, "Is this it?" and Tsitctinako answered yes or no. In that way they identified the four seeds and then buried them in their underground world. All the trees sprouted, but they grew very slowly in the dark. The women themselves slept for a long time, and whenever they woke, they felt the trees to find out how tall they were. A certain pine grew faster than the others, and after a very long time, it pushed a hole through the earth and let in a little light.

The shaft of light reached into the place where the two sisters lived. "It is time for you to go out," Tsitctlnako said. "When you come to the top, wait for the sun to rise. That direction is called *ha'nami*, east. Pray to the sun with pollen and sacred cornmeal, which you will find in your baskets. Thank the sun for bringing you light. Ask for long life and happiness and for success in the purposes for which you were created."

Tsitctinako taught them the prayers to say and the creation song to sing. Then the sisters climbed up the pine tree. Stepping out into the light, the sisters put down their baskets and for the first time saw what they contained. Gradually the sky grew lighter, and finally the sun came up. As they faced it, their eyes hurt, for they were not accustomed to the bright light.

ABOVE: A partial enactment of the myth of Tsitctinako, the Corn Dance was performed by many cultures in the southwest where corn made up nearly eighty percent of the inhabitants' diet.

LEFT: This pottery jar from the Acoma Pueblo culture displays several mythic creatures, including the roadrunner and the deer.

Before they began to pray, Tsitctinako told them that their right side, the side their best arm was on, would be known as south, and the left north. At their backs was west, the direction in which the sun would go down. Underground they had already learned the direction *nuk'um'*, or down.

As they waited to pray to the sun, the girl on the right moved her best hand and was named Ia'tik, which means "Bringing-to-life." "Now name your sister," Tsitctinako told her. Ia'tik was perplexed at first, but then she noticed that her sister's basket was fuller than her own. So she called her sister Nao'tsiti—"More-of-everything-in-the-basket."

The sisters prayed and sang the creation song, and for the first time they asked Tsitctinako why they had been created. The spirit replied, "It was not I but your father, Utc'tsiti, who made you. He made the world, the sun, the sky, and many other things, but he is not yet satisfied. For this reason he has made you in his image. You will rule over the world and create the things he has given you in the baskets."

"From now on," Tsitctinako told the sisters, "you will rule in every direction, north, west, south, and east. Bring everything in your baskets to life, for Utc'tsiti has created you to help him complete the world. Now is the time to plant the seeds."

So far the sisters had not eaten food, and they did not understand what the seeds in their baskets were for. "First plant the corn, and when it grows, it will produce a part that you can eat," Tsitctinako said. Highly interested, the two women watched the growing corn every day. After a while the corn turned hard and ripe. Ia'tik and Nao'tsiti carefully picked two ears without hurting the plant. Tsitctinako had said that the corn must be cooked, but the sisters did not understand what "cooked" meant until a red light fell from the sky that evening. Explaining that it was fire, the spirit taught them to scoop up some flames onto a flat rock and feed themselves with branches from the pine tree.

Following Tsitctinako's direction, they roasted the corn and seasoned it with salt from their baskets. Nao'tsiti grabbed some and ate it, proclaiming how good it was. Then she gave a piece to Ia'tik, and so it was that the two women had their first meal. "You have been fasting for a long time, and your father has nourished you," the spirit told them. "Now you will eat in order to live."

Then Tsitctinako taught them how to sing songs in order to create animals, and the sisters sang and sang. First, they created rodents, like mice and rats and prairie dogs; then they created rabbits, jackrabbits, and antelope; then deer and elk and mountain sheep. Then they sang and created mountain lions, wolves, bobcats, and bears; then eagles and hawks and owls. Then finally they sang and created fish and turtles and snakes. So finally everything was as it should be.

Showing a man and bear wrestling to the death, this southwestern ceramic bowl would have been used ceremonially to commemorate the dead person's spirit, which was released through the hole chipped in the center.

HOW THE PEOPLE BEGAN: STORIES OF THE ORIGINS OF CULTURE AND OF CEREMONIES AND RITUALS

Although Native Americans have many tales of the world's creation, they tend to be more interested in stories explaining the origins of cultural practices and ceremonies. These stories are told more often, and exist in greater variety, than almost any other category of tale. Here, as in the physical creation stories, there are often pairs of twins who define and create the customs by which people live. Sometimes it is not a set of twins but a single child. More common than even

More important to Native American cultures than stories of physical creation, myths concerning the origins of people, as well as their customs and rituals, were told and cherished by the young and old alike.

this are the female deities who visit and teach the hapless humans. The common thread among all the stories is that the teachers of these rituals and ceremonies are themselves supernatural, having great power that they usually get directly from nature itself. Likewise the rituals and ceremonies are almost always designed to pay homage to and celebrate nature and the power within it.

Many ancient tribal teachers are female, especially among plains tribes, even though the tribes' social structures are dominated by men. Perhaps women are perceived to be more closely tied to nature and therefore more appropriate teachers of reverence toward nature, or perhaps the teaching figure needs to be associated with the forces of fertility and childbirth. For whatever reason, the teacher is usually a young woman, though on rare occasions the teacher will be male, typically a male child. In addition, the Trickster is often depicted as having a hand in the origin of human ceremonies.

This first tale comes from the Lakota nation, a confederation of seven tribes inhabiting the northern great plains. This story has been recorded in many versions, including one that appears in John (Fire) Lame Deer's autobiography titled *Lame Deer: Seeker of Visions* (1972) and another told by Henry Crow Dog and recorded by Richard Erdoes in *American Indian Myths and Legends* (1984). Most plains tribes, even those not culturally affiliated with the Lakota, had a similar tale of a young boy who rescues his uncles and thereby begins the ritual of the sweat lodge. A sweat lodge is a small tepeelike structure into which people crouch in a circle. Hot stones are placed in the center of the circle, and a holy man sprinkles water on the rocks, creating steam, which purifies the participants. Sweat baths were common across the continent and were usually considered a necessary preliminary before any other rituals could proceed.

This Lakota man, emerging from a sweat lodge, has participated in a sacred ceremony that began with the young hero Stone Boy who rescued his uncles and restored them to life. Stone Boy did this by following the instructions of his brothers, the stones, to heat them, cover them in a hide lodge, and sprinkle water on them to create steam, the breath of life.

ABOVE: Holding a traditional Eagle Feather fan, this Lakota man lives in a world organized through the mythology that surrounds him. Stories about such figures as Stone Boy reveal the roots of the Lakota religion and the values the people live by.

OPPOSITE: The pipe is the most sacred icon in the Lakota religion, measuring the bounty of the earth, represented by the kinnickinnick or red willow tree bark tobacco and the red pipestone and wood that formed the pipe itself, and the bounty of the spirits, represented by the smoke that rises to the sky and the breath that gives us life.

THE STORY OF IYA HOKSHI, THE STONE BOY

[LAKOTA]

Back in the early days of the Indians, before there were any ceremonies, a young girl, a *winchinchala*, and her five brothers lived together. Once, because they were looking for food, this family moved their tepee to the bottom of a canyon. It was a strange and scary place full of noises, but there was water in a creek and the hunting was good. The canyon was cool in the summer and shielded from wind in the winter. Still when the brothers went out hunting, the girl was scared. She heard noises while she waited for them. Then one evening, only four of the five brothers came back from hunting. They and the sister

stayed awake all night, wondering what could have happened to the other brother. The next day when the men went hunting, only three returned. Again they and the sister stayed awake wondering. The next evening only two came home, and they and the girl were very afraid.

Again the brothers went out in the morning, and only a single one returned at night. Now the girl cried and begged him to stay home. But they had to eat, and so in the morning her last and youngest brother, whom she loved best of all, went out to hunt. Like the others, he did not come back. Now no one would bring the young girl food or water or protect her.

Weeping, the girl left the canyon and climbed to the top of a hill. She wanted to commit suicide, but she did not know how to do such a thing. Then she saw a round pebble lying on the ground. Thinking that it would kill her if she ate it, she picked it up and swallowed it.

The next day she had nothing left to eat except some pemmican and berries. She meant to eat some of her food and drink water from the creek, but she found she wasn't hungry. In fact she felt as if she had been to a feast, and she walked around singing to herself all day.

On the fourth day that the girl had been alone, she felt pain. "Now death will finally come," she thought. "It is finally my time to die." She didn't really mind dying because she missed her brothers. But instead of dying, she gave birth to a little boy.

"What will I do with this child?" she wondered. "How did I give birth? It must have something to do with that stone I swallowed. Yes, he looks like a stone boy in the face."

The child was strong, with shining eyes. Though the girl felt weak for a while, she had to keep going to care for the new child. She named him Iya Hokshi, Stone Boy, and

wrapped him in her brothers' clothes. Day after day he grew, ten times faster than ordinary babies, and with a more perfect body.

The mother knew that her baby had great powers. One day when he was playing outside the tepee, he made a bow and arrows, all on his own. The baby grew so fast that he was soon walking. His hair became long, and as he matured his mother became afraid that she would lose him as she had lost her brothers. Very soon he was big enough to go hunting, and when she saw this, his mother began to weep loudly.

"You used to have five uncles," she told her son, sobbing. "But they went out hunting. One after another they did not come back." And she told him about his birth, how she had gone to the top of the hill and there swallowed a stone.

"I know," he said. "And I am going to look for your brothers, my uncles."

So the next morning Iya Hokshi started walking and watching. He wandered for four days, and on the evening of the fourth day he smelled smoke. It led him to a tepee with smoke coming from its smoke hole.

This tepee was ugly and ramshackle. Inside Iya Hokshi could see an old ugly woman. She looked like a witch to Iya Hokshi. She watched him pass and, calling him over, invited him to eat and stay the night.

Stone Boy entered the tepee, though he was uneasy in his mind and a bit timid. Looking around, he saw five big bundles, propped on end, leaning against the tepee wall. He wondered if those might be his uncles.

The old woman was cooking some meat. When it was done he ate it, though it didn't taste good. Later she fixed a dirty old buffalo robe for him to sleep on, but he sensed danger and felt wide awake.

"I have a backache," the woman said. "Before you go to sleep, I wish you would ease it for me by walking up and down my back. I am old and alone, and I have nobody to help me with my pain."

OPPOSITE: This painting, on display at the Rockwell Museum in Corning, New York, shows one of the many uses the Lakota had for fire and smoke. Not only was fire sacred, it was essential for warmth, for tool making, and for cooking. It was also used here as a form of communication over long distances; the length and shape of the billowing smoke formed a standard signal that could be read for miles.

BELOW: The forbidding landscape of the South Dakota Badlands region functioned as an impressive backdrop to many of the Lakotas' earliest stories, with the landscape itself often playing a vital and active role in the tales that featured it.

Like their western cousins the Lakotas, the Ting-ta-to-ah Band of Eastern Dakotas began their culture around the Great Lakes in what is now Minnesota and Wisconsin. Many of their myths reflect life in these great northern forests.

She lay down, and Stone Boy began walking on her back. As he did, he felt something sticking up under her buckskin robe, something sharp like a knife or a needle or the point of a spear. "Maybe she used this sharp tool to kill my uncles," he thought. "Maybe she put poison from a snake on its point. Yes, that must be what happened."

Iya Hokshi, having pondered enough, jumped high in the air, as high as he could, and came down on that old woman's back with a crash. He jumped and jumped until he was exhausted, and the old witch was lying dead with a broken back.

Then Iya Hokshi walked over to the big bundles, which were wrapped in animal hides and lashed together with rawhide thongs. He unwrapped them and found five men, dead and dried like jerky meat, hardly human-looking. "These must be my uncles," he thought, but he didn't know how to bring them back to life.

Outside the ugly tepee was a heap of round gray stones. He found that they were talking and that he could understand them. "Iya Hokshi, Stone Boy, you are one of us, you come from us, you come from Tunka, you come from Iya. Listen. Pay attention, and do what we tell you."

Following their instructions, he built a little domelike hut out of bent willow sticks. He covered it with the old witch's buffalo robes and put the five dead, dried-up humans inside. Out in the open he built a big fire. He set the rocks right in the flames, picked up the old witch, and threw her in to burn up.

After the rocks glowed red hot, Stone Boy found a deer antler and used it to carry them one by one into the little hut he had made. He picked up the old witch's water bag, a buffalo bladder decorated with quillwork, and filled it with water. He drew its rawhide tie tight and took it inside too. Then he placed the dried humans around him in a circle.

Iya Hokshi closed the entrance of his little lodge with a flap of buffalo robe so that no air could escape or enter. Pouring water from the bag over them, he thanked the rocks, saying, "You brought me here." Four times he poured the water. Four times he opened the flap and closed it. Always he spoke to the rocks and they to him. As he poured, the little lodge filled with steam so that he could see nothing but the white mist in the darkness. When he poured water a second time, he sensed a stirring. When he poured the third time, he began to sing. And when he poured the fourth time, those dead, dried-up things also began to talk and then to sing.

"I believe they have come back to life," thought Iya Hokshi. "Now I will finally get to meet my uncles."

He opened the flap for the last time, watching the steam flow out and rise into the sky as a feathery cloud. The fire and the moonlight both shone into the little sweat lodge, and by their light he saw five handsome young men sitting inside. He said, "You must be my uncles." They smiled and laughed, happy to be alive again.

Iya Hokshi then said, "The rock saved me, and now it has saved you. We will learn to worship Iya, Tunka—rock—and Tunkashila—the Grandfather Spirit. This little lodge, these rocks, the water, the fire—these are sacred, these we will use from now on as we have done here for the first time: for purification, for life, for health. This is the first *inipi* ceremony, the first sweat bath ceremony. This has been given to us so that we may live. We shall now become a tribe."

•

Native American tribes often attribute their own origins to the origins of the plants or animals they primarily subsist on. This tale comes from the Penobscot tribe of New England, and highlights the sacrifices made by the ancestors. Variations of the same story are told throughout the southern and southwestern regions as well; one version is included in Joseph Nicolar's *The Life and Traditions of the Red Man* (1893).

FIRST MOTHER GIVES THE GIFT OF CORN

[PENOBSCOT]

When Kloskurbeh, the one who made everything, lived on earth, there were no people yet. But one day, when the sun was high, a young man appeared and called him "Uncle, brother of my mother." This young man was born from the foam of the waves, foam stirred up by the wind and warmed by the sun. It was the motion of the wind, the moistness of wa-

To the Natives of North America, whether in the southwest or the northeast, corn represented the staple of life. Its nutritious grain, hardy nature, and unusual versatility made it the ideal food for most tribes. Many legends and myths feature corn or corn beings.

ter, and the sun's warmth that gave him life—warmth above all, because warmth is life. And the young man lived with Kloskurbeh and became his chief helper.

Now after these two powerful beings had created all manner of things, there came to them, as the sun was shining at high noon, a beautiful girl. She was born of the wonderful earth plants, and of the dew, and of warmth. Because a drop of dew fell on a leaf and was warmed by the sun, and the warming sun is life, this girl came into being—from the green living plant, from moisture, and from warmth.

"I am love," said the maiden. "I am a strength giver, I am the nourisher, I am the provider of men and animals."

Then Kloskurbeh thanked the Great Mystery Above for having sent them the young girl. The youth, the Great Nephew, married her, and the girl conceived and thus became First Mother. And Kloskurbeh, the Great Uncle, who teaches humans all they need to know, taught their children how to live. Then he went away to dwell in the north.

Now the people increased and became numerous. They lived by hunting, and the more people there were, the less game they found. They were hunting too much, and as the animals decreased, starvation came upon the people. And First Mother pitied them.

The little children came to First Mother and said, "We are hungry. Feed us." But she had nothing to give them, and she wept. She told them, "Be patient. I will make some food. Then your little bellies will be full." But she kept weeping.

Her husband asked, "How can I make you smile? How can I make you happy?"

"There is only thing that will stop my tears."

"What is it?" asked her husband.

"Husband, you must kill me."

"I could never do that."

"You must, or I will go on weeping and grieving forever."

Then the husband traveled far, to the end of the earth, to the north he went, to ask the Great Instructor, his uncle Kloskurbeh, what he should do.

"You must do what she wants. You must kill her," said Kloskurbeh. Then the young man went back to his home, and it was his turn to weep. But First Mother said, "Tomorrow at high noon you must do it. After you have killed me, let two of our sons take hold of my hair and drag my body over that empty patch of earth. Let them drag me back and forth, back and forth, over every part of the patch, until all my flesh has been torn from my body. Afterward take my bones, gather them up, and bury them in the middle of this patch. Then leave that place."

She smiled and said, "Wait seven months and then come back, and you will find my flesh there, flesh given out of love, and it will nourish and strengthen you forever and ever."

So it was done. The husband slew his wife. Then her sons, praying, dragged her body back and forth just as she had commanded, until her flesh covered the whole patch of earth. Finally, they took up her bones and buried them in the middle of it. Weeping loudly, they went away.

When the husband and his children and his children's children came back to that place after seven months had passed, they found the ground covered with tall, green, tasseled plants. The plants' fruit—corn—was First Mother's flesh, given so that the people might live and flourish. And they ate of First Mother's flesh and found it sweet indeed. Following her instructions, they did not eat it all, but put many kernels back into the earth. In this way her flesh and spirit renewed themselves every seven months, generation after generation.

And at the spot where they had buried First Mother's bones, there grew another plant, broad-leafed and fragrant. It was First Mother's breath, and they heard her spirit talking: "Burn this up and smoke it. It is sacred. It will clear your minds, help your prayers, and gladden your hearts." And First

Mother's husband called the first plant *skarmunal*, corn, and the second plant *utarmurwayeh*, tobacco.

"Remember," he told the people, "and take good care of First Mother's flesh, because it is her goodness that has become substance. Take good care of her breath, because it is her love turned into smoke. Remember her and think of her whenever you eat, whenever you smoke this sacred plant, because she has given her life so that you might live. Yet she is not herself dead, she lives. In undying love she renews herself again and again every seven months."

Along with corn, or First Mother's flesh, tobacco represented one of the most sacred plants to the Penobscot tribe, representing First Mother's breath. If First Mother's flesh nourished their bodies, her breath, in the form of tobacco, nourished their spirit.

OUR BROTHERS, THE FOUR-LEGGED AND TWO-LEGGED: STORIES OF ANIMALS AND ANIMAL ORIGINS

Most Native American stories feature animal characters or Trickster figures in the form of animals. The European tradition includes similar stories, myths, and fables featuring animal characters that are used to illustrate a moral lesson or, perhaps, display some form of folk wisdom. Native cultures used animal stories in much the same way.

Whether it's a legend about why crows are black, about some conflict between animals that carved a particular feature of the landscape, or connecting

---

All Native American cultures paid homage to the living creatures around them. Stories about animals and animal origins were, without a doubt, the most often repeated and most well known type of story among Indian peoples.

From the Tsimshian tribe in the northwest region, this button-blanket illustrates a council gathering similar to the council described in the story "The Gathering of the Wild Animals."

animal behavior and actions to features in the night sky, each story involving animals is sure to contain a moral lesson, to illustrate a truth about human behavior. Just as European fables use animals to depict human emotions and the human concepts, of right and wrong in our traditions, Native American stories use animals to demonstrate both proper behavior and the consequences of greed and mean-spiritedness.

Sometimes, however, animal stories are about the animals themselves, illustrating the dangers certain animals present, or teaching the proper ways to approach certain animals. Many of these stories involve the etiquette of the hunter, the trapper, and the fisherman, demonstrating the necessary rituals involved and explaining their origins.

At other times, these stories illustrate the interdependence of Native American societies and their animal counterparts. Tales of this type usually involve a marriage between a human character and an animal, and usually these unions produce children that reinforce these connections and bonds. Often because of these legends, certain tribes would identify themselves with a particular totem animal, such as the bear, the buffalo, or the deer. Stories of human and animal marriages, then, serve to strengthen these bonds and to demonstrate the kinship and respect that native peoples have for their animal cousins and for nature in general.

This first story comes from the Tsimshian tribe, whose origins are in the Pacific northwest, and was recorded by the anthropologist

Franz Boas in *Tsimshian Mythology* (1916). Similar stories are told throughout the region, however, as well as in many other regions. One of its interesting features is that it depicts animals employing a collective decision-making process as they try to cope with the devastation Tsimshian hunters are causing to their numbers.

THE GATHERING
OF THE WILD
ANIMALS

[TSIMSHIAN]

Grizzly Bear invited all the large animals to his lodge. "A terrible disaster has come to us with these hunting people, the Tsimshian, those great hunters who pursue us even into our dens," he said. "I suggest we ask Him-Who-Made-Us to give us more cold winter and keep the hunters in their own houses and out of our dens!" All the large animals agreed, and Wolf said, "Let's invite all the small animals—Porcupine, Beaver, Raccoon, Marten, Mink, and even the really small ones such as Mouse and the insects—to join us and increase our strength so that Him-Who-Made-Us will listen to our plea."

The next day the large animals assembled on a wide prairie and called together all the small animals, even the insects. The multitude sat down, with the small animals on one side, the large animals on the other.

Then the first speaker, Grizzly Bear, rose. "Friends," he said to the small animals and the insects, "you know very well how the Tsimshian people hunt us on mountains and hills, even pursuing us into our dens. Therefore, my brothers, we large animals have agreed to ask Him-Who-Made-Us to give our

earth cold winters, colder than ever, so that the people who hunt us cannot come to our dens and kill us—or you! Large animals, is this what we decided?"

Panther said, "I fully support this wise counsel," and all the large animals agreed. Grizzly Bear turned to the small animals and said, "We want to know what you think in this matter." The small animals did not reply at first. After they had been silent for a while, Porcupine rose and said, "Friends, let me say a word or two in response. Your strategy is very good for you, because all of you have plenty

The great grizzly bear of North America represented to many tribes, including the Tsimshian, physical power, strength of character, and leadership. And yet, though Bear is often described as wise, he can also sometimes be too hasty in his conclusions and somewhat selfish.

This wooden Tsimshian mask, carved in 1885, was used in tribal ceremonies and gatherings. It was usually carried by the leader of the clan it represented as the members approached the gathering site.

of warm fur for the most severe winter. But look at these little insects. They have no fur at all to warm them in the cold. Moreover, how can insects and small animals obtain food if winters are colder? Therefore I say, don't ask for more cold winter." Then he sat down.

Grizzly Bear rose again. "We need not pay attention to what Porcupine says," he told the large animals. "You all agree, don't you, that we should ask for the severest cold on earth?" The large animals replied, "Yes, we do. We don't care for Porcupine's reasoning."

"Now listen once more! I will ask you just one question," Porcupine said. "If it's that cold, the roots of all the wild berries will freeze and die, and all the plants of the prairie will wither away. How will you get food? You large animals always roam the land wanting something to eat. When your request brings more winter frost, you will die of starvation.

But we will survive, for we live on the bark of trees, the very small animals eat the gum of trees, and the smallest insects find their food in the earth."

The large animals were speechless at Porcupine's wisdom. Finally Grizzly Bear admitted, "It might be true what you have said." And the large animals chose Porcupine as their wise man and as the first among the small animals. Together all the animals agreed that the cold in winter should last six months, and there should be six months for summer.

Then Porcupine spoke again in his wisdom: "In winter we will have ice and snow. In spring we will have showers, and the plants will become green. In summer we will have warmer weather, and all the fishes will go up the rivers. In fall the leaves will drop, it will rain, and the rivers and brooks will overflow. Then all the animals, large and small, and those that creep on the ground will go into their dens and hide for six months." And after they all agreed to what Porcupine had said, they all happily returned to their homes.

•

The next story comes from the Creek tribe, a southeastern group who originally lived in what is now middle and southern Georgia. In the southeast, Rabbit is often synonymous with Trickster, although here he is portrayed merely as a simple, though tricky and conniving, animal who learns the consequences of cheating. Many versions of this story exist, including a similar Cherokee tale recorded by James Mooney in *Myths of the Cherokee* (1902).

HOW RABBIT'S TRICK GOT DEER HIS ANTLERS

[CREEK]

In the beginning Deer had no antlers, and his head was smooth just like a doe's. He was a great runner, while Rabbit was a great jumper, and the animals were all curious to know which of the two could go farther in the same amount of time. They talked about it a good deal, and at last they arranged a race between the two and made a nice large pair of antlers as a prize for the winner. They were to start together from one side of a thicket and go through it, then turn and come back, and the one who came out first would get the antlers.

On the day of the race, all the animals were there, with the antlers put down on the ground at the edge of the thicket to mark the starting point. While everybody was admiring the antlers Rabbit said, "I don't know this country very well. I want to take a look

through the bushes where I am supposed to run." They thought that was all right, so Rabbit went into the thicket, but he was gone so long that at last the animals suspected he must be up to one of his tricks. They sent a messenger, who found Rabbit gnawing down the bushes and pulling them away until he had a path cleared nearly to the other side.

The messenger turned around quietly and came back and told the other animals. When Rabbit came out at last they accused him of

To the Creek, as well as the Cherokee, the Catawba, and other southeastern tribes, Rabbit functioned as the epitome of flawed values. He represented treachery, guile, dishonesty, and cowardice.

HOW OWL
GOT BIG EYES

[IROQUOIS]

Raweno, the maker of everything, was busy creating all the animals. He was working on Rabbit, and Rabbit was saying, "I want nice long legs and long ears like Deer and sharp fangs and claws like Panther."

"I do them up the way they want to be," said Raweno. "I give them what they ask for." He was working on Rabbit's hind legs, making them long, the way Rabbit had ordered.

Owl, who was still unformed, was sitting on a tree nearby and waiting his turn. He was saying, "Whoo, whoo, whoo, I want a nice long neck like Swan's, and beautiful red feath-

ABOVE: A southeastern group known for their fierceness in battle, the Creek nation delighted in tales of cunning, devious schemes and their questionable outcomes. The Creek prized honest, straightforward competition, so the trickster figure Rabbit is usually not rewarded for his deceptions in the Creek stories.

RIGHT: Painstakingly woven and elaborately designed, baskets such as this one are beautiful artistic expressions of Iroquois art and culture.

cheating, but he denied it until they went into the thicket and found the cleared path. They agreed that such a Trickster had no right to enter the race at all, so they gave the antlers to Deer, who was from then on said to be the best runner; he has worn those antlers proudly ever since. They told Rabbit that because he was so fond of cutting down bushes, he might do that from then on, and so he gnaws bushes for a living to this day.

•

In yet another animal origin story, recorded by several nineteenth- and twentieth-century ethnographers, the Iroquois, a confederation of tribes that inhabited parts of Ontario, Quebec, and upstate New York, tell of the origin of Owl, an animal they thought to be im-

The Iroquois believed
in the god Raweno,
the maker of all
things, who, because
he embodied great
wisdom, fashioned
each creature—
even man—according
to that creature's
inner nature.

ers like Cardinal's, and a nice long beak like Egret's, and a nice crown of plumes like Heron's. I want you to make me into the most beautiful, the fastest, and the most wonderful of all the birds."

Raweno said, "Be quiet. Turn around and look in another direction. Even better, close your eyes. Don't you know that no one is allowed to watch me work?" Raweno was just then making Rabbit's ears very long, the way Rabbit wanted them.

Owl refused to do what Raweno said. "Whoo, whoo, whoo," he replied, "nobody can forbid me to watch. Nobody can order me to close my eyes. I like watching you, and watch I will."

Then Raweno became angry. He grabbed Owl, pulling him down from his branch, stuffing his head deep into his body, shaking him until his eyes grew big with fright, pulling at his ears until they were sticking up on both sides of his head.

ABOVE: According to Iroquois legend, these barn owls received their body shape and their distinctive heads and eyes because of their impatient and rude natures.

"There," said Raweno, "that'll teach you. Now you won't be able to crane your neck to watch things that you shouldn't watch. Now you have big ears to listen when someone tells you what you shouldn't do. And now you have big eyes—but not so big that you can watch me, because you'll be awake only at night, and I work by day. And your feathers won't be red like Cardinal's but gray like this"—and Raweno rubbed Owl all over with mud—"as punishment for your disobedience," he said. So Owl flew off, pouting, "Whoo, whoo, whoo."

Then Raweno turned back to finish with Rabbit, but Rabbit had been so terrified by Raweno's anger, even though it was not directed at him, that he ran off before he was finished. Because of this, only Rabbit's hind legs are long, and he has to hop about instead of walking and running. Also because he became scared at that moment, Rabbit has remained afraid of almost everything, and he never got the claws and fangs he had asked for to defend himself. Had he not run away then, Rabbit would have been an altogether different animal.

LEFT: Iroquois children were especially fond of animal stories, and would learn what sort of behavior and ethical values their culture expected from them by hearing about the antics of Owl, Beaver, and Deer.

OPPOSITE, BOTTOM: Serving as totems for clan affiliation, animals represented traits and strengths that their respective clans emulated. People born into a clan were said to embody the traits of their totem animal, or perhaps were spiritually guided by them.

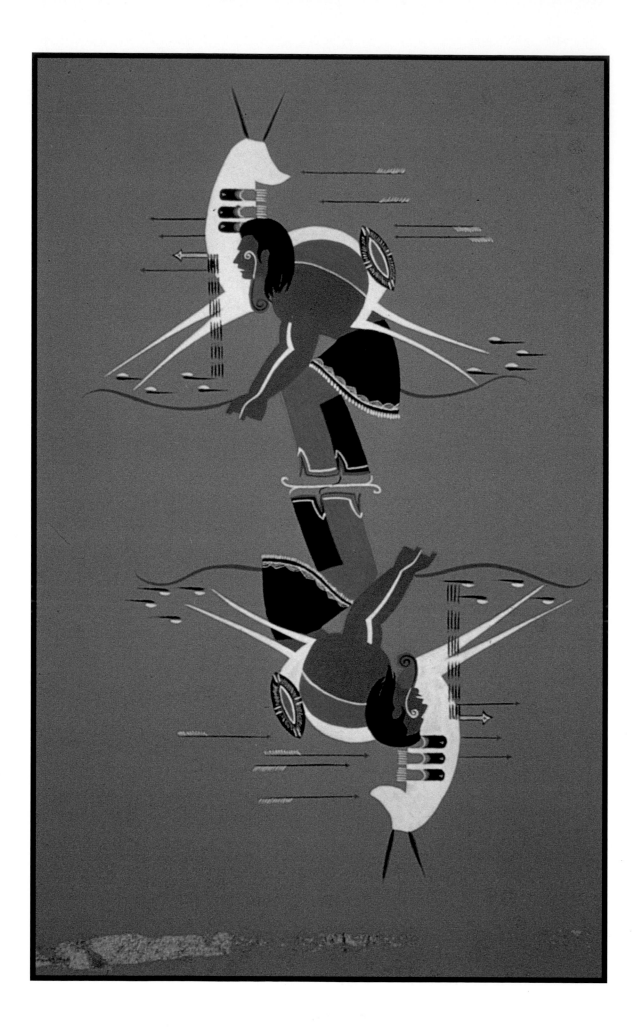

THE BEST THAT IS IN US ALL: STORIES OF THE HERO

These tales are related to stories of war and the warrior code, though generally speaking, war stories are about authentic episodes in the real lives of warriors, while stories of heroes are much more stylized in form, mythic in their scope, and, for the most part, supernatural in their content. As in the European tradition, Native American hero myths are full of dragons, giants, monsters of all description, demons, ogres, and witches. The hero, of course, battles these horrors and abominations of nature using a variety of methods

Whether their status came from fantastic prowess against an enemy,
from killing a dreaded monster, or from their role as exemplary
hunters and providers, Native American heroes served as role models
for their people, expressing the best that humanity could aspire to.

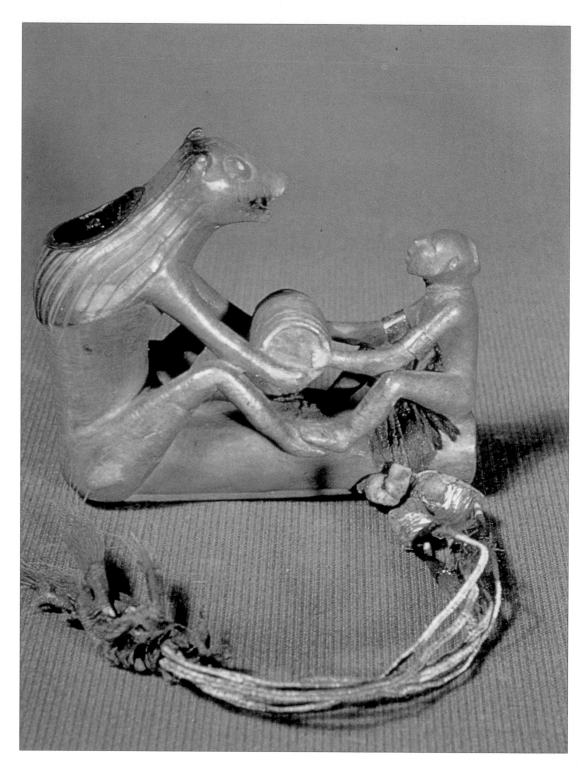

and skills, depending on the tribe originating the myth. Depending on the tribe, as well, the hero myth may not even stand alone as a distinct type of story but will sometimes merge with creation stories or stories of cultural origins that explain how a hero caused a thing to come about or a tradition to start.

Some abilities or traits are shared by the heroes of different tribes and tribal groups.

Most heroes can change their shape at will, especially into any animal form, and they can almost universally speak to the animals they encounter. Indeed, the hero is often referred to as an animal, or as a man in an-imal shape, such as Old Man Coyote or Great Bear Man. Most have the power of invisibility, being able either to hide without being seen or to misdirect the eyes of their enemies. Heroes almost always have a mysterious birth, or an unusual or supernatural conception, such as a maiden being impregnated in a dream or a swallowed rock causing pregnancy. Another nearly universal quality of Native American heroes is their decidedly human nature, including weaknesses or appetites that interfere with their supernatural powers.

The tasks that Native American heroes accomplish are often large and mythic in scope, such as a great battle with a huge gluttonous monster who has a craving for young Indian maidens or with giant animals who guard secret places, or great trials involving all the elements that a warrior might fear, such as terrible storms, surging waters, or raging fires.

The trials heroes face are remarkably similar across the continent. Nearly all tribes living in the Great Lakes region or along the coasts tell of giant water monsters, which the Lakota called Unktehi and the Ojibwa called Missuppishu, whose bones could be found in the ground in the Badlands of South Dakota. Most tribes also have stories of No Body, a huge head that rolls along, crushing everything in its path, or grotesque animals such as Delgeth, a huge antelope or deer who eats flesh and kills people for the sport of it. These are the monsters the hero has to fight, and as in the European tradition, the specific nature of a given hero's talent gives great insight into what each society believed was valuable in human behavior, what traits its members should aspire to have, and what values they should hold dear.

This first tale, retold from a variety of nineteenth- and twentieth-century sources, features the hero Glooscap, the superwarrior of the Algonquin tribes of the northeast. This particular story comes from the Micmac tribe, who lived in what is now the Canadian Maritime provinces. It combines many of the elements discussed above, and it is part of a larger creation story.

GLOOSCAP CONFRONTS THE WATER MONSTER

[MICMAC]

Glooscap is a spirit warrior, a holy man, a sorcerer. He can do anything. Once he started a village and taught the people there everything they needed to know to be happy. And the people were happy. They were happy hunting and fishing. Men and women were happy making love. Children were happy playing. Parents cherished their children, and children respected their parents. All was just the way Glooscap wanted it.

The village had one spring, the only source of water far and wide, that always flowed with pure, clear, cold water. But one day the spring ran dry. Only a little bit of slimy ooze flowed from it. It stayed dry even in the fall when the rains came, and in the spring when the snows melted. The people wondered, "What shall we do? We can't live without water." The wise men and elders held a council and decided to send a man north to the source of the spring to see why it had suddenly run dry.

The Micmac, a large Algonqian tribe in southeastern Canada, were known for their quilled beadwork. This small box was made in the nineteenth century.

The man they chose walked a long time until at last he came to a village. The people there were not human beings. They looked something like us, but they had webbed hands and feet. At this village, the brook widened out. There was some water in it—not much, but a little—though it was slimy, yellowish, and stinking. The man was thirsty from his walk and asked to be given a little water, even if it was bad.

"We can't give you any water," said the people with the webbed hands and feet, "unless our great chief permits it. He wants all the water for himself."

"Where is your chief?" asked the man.

"You must follow the brook further up," they told him.

The man walked on and at last met the big chief. When he saw him he trembled with fright, because the chief was a monster so huge that if one stood at his feet, one could not see his head. The monster filled the whole valley from end to end. He had dug himself a huge hole and dammed it up so that all the water was in it and none could flow into the stream bed. And he had fouled the water and made it poisonous, so that stinking mists hovered above its slimy surface.

The monster had a huge, grinning mouth going from ear to ear. His dull yellow eyes started out of his head like huge pine knots. His body was bloated and covered with warts as big as mountains. The monster stared dully at the man with his protruding eyes and finally said in a fearsome croak, "Little man, what do you want?"

The man was terrified, but he said, "I come from a village far downstream. Our only spring ran dry, because you're keeping all the water for yourself. We would like you to let us have some of this water."

The monster blinked at him a few times. Finally he croaked, "Do as you please, I don't care, but if you want water, go elsewhere!"

The man then said, "We need the water. The people are dying of thirst." The monster replied, "I don't care. Don't bother me. Go away, or I'll swallow you up!"

The monster opened his mouth wide from ear to ear, and inside it the man could see the many things that the creature had killed. The monster gulped a few times and

Living in small, wigwam-style thatched dwellings, the Micmac occupied what is now Maine, New Brunswick, Nova Scotia, and Newfoundland.

smacked his lips with a noise like thunder. At this the man's courage broke, and he turned and ran away as fast as he could.

Now Glooscap knows everything that goes on in the world, even before it happens. So when he knew of his people's plight, he said to himself, "I must set things right. I'll have to get water for my people!"

So Glooscap made himself ready for war. He painted his body with paint as red as blood. He made himself twelve feet tall. He used two huge clamshells for his earrings. He put a hundred black eagle feathers and a hundred white eagle feathers in his scalp lock. He painted yellow rings around his eyes. He twisted his mouth into a snarl and made himself look ferocious. He stamped, and the earth trembled. He uttered his fearful war cry, and it echoed and reechoed from all the mountains. He grasped a huge mountain in his hand, a mountain composed of flint, and from it made himself a single knife as sharp as a weasel's teeth. "Now I am going," he said, striding ahead, with mighty eagles circling above him. Thus Glooscap came to the village of the people with the webbed hands and feet.

"I want water," he told them. Looking at him, they were afraid. They brought him a little muddy water. "I think I'll get more and cleaner water," he said. Glooscap went upstream and confronted the monster. "I want clean water," he said, "and a lot of it, for the people downstream."

The monster then said, "Ho! Ho! All the waters are mine! Go away! Or I'll kill you!"

"Slimy pile of mud!" cried Glooscap. "We'll see who will be killed!" They fought. The mountains shook. The earth split open. The swamp smoked and burst into flames. Mighty trees were shivered into splinters.

The monster opened its huge mouth wide to swallow Glooscap. Glooscap made himself taller than the tallest tree, and even the monster's mile-wide mouth was too small for him.

Glooscap seized his great flint knife and slit the monster's bloated belly. From the wound gushed a mighty stream, a roaring river, tumbling, rolling, foaming down, down, down, gouging out for itself a vast, deep bed, flowing by the village and on to the great sea in the east.

"That should be enough water for the people," said Glooscap. Then he grasped the monster and squeezed him in his mighty palm, flinging him at last into the swamp. Glooscap had squeezed this great creature into a small bullfrog, and ever since the bullfrog's skin has been wrinkled because Glooscap squeezed so hard. The bullfrog's tribe of people with webbed hands and feet became frogs as well, and lived ever after in the waters that Glooscap had formed.

•

This next story comes from the Iroquois, who formed a confederation of tribes known as the Five Nations, consisting of the Mohawks, the Oneidas, the Onondagas, the Cayugas, and the Senecas. It is the story of Hiawatha and his efforts to unite the Iroquois against a common enemy.

HIAWATHA THE PEACEMAKER

[IROQUOIS]

One of the greatest Iroquois stories tells of the peacemaking leader Hiawatha, who united the five tribes that made up the Iroquois league and brought a system of government that was so equitable that many historians believe it may have served as the model for the American form of government.

Ta-ren-ya-wa-gon, the Great-Upholder-of-the-Heavens, once decided to live among the people as a human being. Having the power to make himself into any shape, he chose to be a man and took the name of Hiawatha. He chose to live among the Onondagas and took a beautiful young girl of that tribe for his wife. From their union came a daughter, Mini-haha, who surpassed even her mother in beauty and womanly skills. Hiawatha never ceased to teach and advise, and above all he preached peace and harmony.

Under Hiawatha, the Onondagas became the greatest of all tribes, but the other nations, the Mohawks, the Oneidas, the Cayugas, and the Senecas, also founded by the Great

Upholder, increased and prospered as well. Traveling in a magic birch-bark canoe of dazzling whiteness, which floated above waters and meadows as if on an invisible bird's wings, Hiawatha went from nation to nation, counseling them and keeping man, animal, and nature in balance according to the eternal laws of the ancestor spirits. So all was well and the people lived happily.

But the law of the universe is also that happiness alternates with sorrow, life with death, prosperity with hardship, harmony with disharmony. From out of the north beyond the Great Lakes came wild tribes, fierce, untutored nations who knew nothing of the eternal law, peoples who did not plant or weave baskets or fire clay into cooking vessels. All they knew was how to prey on those who planted and to reap the fruits of their labor. Fierce and pitiless, these strangers ate their meat raw, tearing it apart with their teeth. Warfare and killing were their only occupations. They burst upon Hiawatha's people like a flood, spreading devastation wherever they went. The people turned to Hiawatha for help. He advised all the nations to assemble and await his coming.

And so the five tribes came together at the place of the great council fire, by the shores of a large and tranquil lake where the wild men from the north had not yet penetrated. The people waited for Hiawatha one day, two days, three days. They began to argue and blame each other for the coming of the fierce, uncivilized people they had to confront. Finally, on the fourth day, Hiawatha's gleaming white, magic canoe appeared, floating, gliding above the mists. Hiawatha sat in the stern guiding the mystery canoe. He stepped ashore and told the people to gather around the council fire.

When the sachems, elders, and wise men had seated themselves in a circle around the sacred fire, Hiawatha came before them and said, "My children, war, fear, and disunity have brought you from your villages to this sacred council fire. Facing a common danger, and fearing for the lives of your families, you have begun to drift apart, each tribe thinking and acting only for itself. You must reunite now and act as one tribe. No single tribe alone can withstand our savage enemies, who care nothing about the eternal laws of the ancestor spirits, who sweep upon us like the storms of winter, spreading death and destruction everywhere. My children, listen well. Remember that you are brothers, that the downfall of one means the downfall of all. You must have one fire, one pipe, one war club."

Hiawatha motioned to the five tribal firekeepers to unite their fires with the big sacred council fire, and they did so. Then the Great Upholder sprinkled sacred tobacco upon the glowing embers so that its sweet fragrance enveloped the wise men sitting in the circle. He said, "Onondagas, you are a tribe of mighty warriors. Your strength is like that of a giant pine tree whose roots spread far and deep so that it can withstand any storm. From now on you be the protectors. You shall be the first nation. Oneidas, your men are famous for their wisdom. You be the counselors of the tribes. You shall be the second nation. Senecas, you are swift of foot and persuasive of speech. Your men are the greatest orators among the tribes. You be the spokesmen for the tribes. You shall be the third people. Cayugas, you are the most cunning people. You are the most skilled in the building and managing of canoes. You be the guardians of our rivers. You

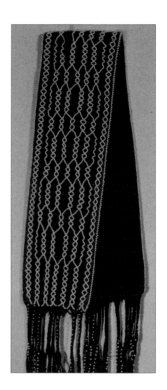

ABOVE: Iroquois beadwork and weaving are known for their intricate design and vibrant colors, as seen in this Seneca sash. The skills of the wampum makers caused their beadwork sashes to be so highly prized that their handiwork was often exchanged in lieu of money.

LEFT: For approximately two hundred years, the League of the Iroquois, founded by Hiawatha (pictured in his canoe in this nineteenth-century engraving), prospered, its peoples living in peace and harmony.

RIGHT: The Iroquois skill of basket-weaving was not merely confined to usable containers. Here a turkey has been woven to honor the bird that provided so much—in terms of food, feathers, and many other usable materials—to these eastern woodland tribes.

BELOW: Like most tribes, the Iroquois used a kind of tobacco, smoking it in gray eastern pipestone bowls carved in a variety of decorative shapes.

OPPOSITE: This Arapaho warrior and his wife display the traditional costumes of their plains culture. Like all midwestern tribal males, the Arapaho men were fierce warriors who lived and died by the "warrior code."

shall be the fourth nation. Mohawks, you are the foremost in planting corn and beans and in building longhouses. You be the nourishers. You five tribes must be like the five fingers of a warrior's hand joined in gripping the war club. Unite as one, and then your enemies will recoil before you back into the northern wastes from whence they came. Let my words sink deep into your hearts and minds. Retire now to take counsel among yourselves, and come to me tomorrow to tell me whether you will follow my advice."

The next morning the sachems and wise men of the five nations came to Hiawatha with the promise that they would from that day on be as one nation. Hiawatha rejoiced. "Henceforth," he said, "you shall be known as the Ako-no-shu-ne, the Iroquois." Thus with the help of Hiawatha, the Great Unifier, the mighty League of the Five Nations was born, and its tribes held sway undisturbed over all the land between the great river of the west and the great sea of the east.

The elders begged Hiawatha to become the chief sachem of the united tribes, but he told them, "This can never be, because I must leave you. Friends and brothers, choose the wisest women in your tribes to be the future clan mothers and peacemakers; let them turn

any strife arising among you into friendship. Let your sachems be wise enough to go to such women for advice when there are disputes. Now I have finished speaking. Farewell."

At that moment there came to those assembled a sweet sound like the rush of rustling leaves and the song of innumerable birds. Hiawatha stepped into his white mystery canoe, and instead of gliding away on the waters of the lake, it rose slowly into the sky and disappeared into the clouds. Hiawatha was gone, but his teaching survives in the hearts of the people.

•

This next tale comes from the Arapaho tribe and was recorded many times in nineteenth- and twentieth-century sources, including one version recorded by George Dorsey and Alfred Kroeber in their work *Traditions of the Arapaho* (1903). It features unusual cannibal monsters with a diminutive human form, similar to monsters found in many European stories, wherein deformed or misshapen individuals are often looked upon with trepidation and fear.

HOW THE CANNIBAL DWARVES WERE KILLED

[ARAPAHO]

Once, a hunter was traveling along the river in search of game. He went up a hill to look for some animal to hunt, but he saw instead a tepee standing by itself. "Somebody is coming, somebody stops at the door, somebody walks from the door, somebody is walking around the tepee, somebody stops at the door and waits to be admitted," said someone inside. So this hunter went in and saw a small dwarf man sitting alone, and he was blind. "Well! Well! You are a very good person bringing yourself in for my food," said the dwarf, moving himself and looking up in the air. He was no dwarf at all, but a cannibal monster who loved strong human flesh.

Of course it is well known that cannibal dwarves are supernatural creatures and that they are very shrewd. But the hunter was more shrewd than this dwarf. He said, "Well,

yes, I came to deliver myself to you. I am very fat and I know that you will relish the meat with your relatives," said the man.

"Thank you! that is what I need," said the dwarf.

"I suppose you are hungry and ready to take me now," said the man.

"Oh, no! I shall wait until my relatives return," said the dwarf.

"All right, I shall wait patiently, too, but excuse me for a short time," said the man, going out. This hunter went and cut a stick, which he sharpened at one end, and went into the tepee with it. "Now, friend, what are these things suspended from the tepee poles?" said the hunter.

"Well, young man, those are hearts belonging to my relatives," said the blind dwarf, "we don't like to carry our hearts when we go out, so we leave them here."

"Well then, friend, can you tell me whose heart this is?" said the hunter, with his sharp stick pointing to one.

"That is my father's heart," said the dwarf. The moment the dwarf told this to the hunter, the hunter punched it with the stick.

All the dwarf's relatives were at that moment out after food. The father dwarf, who

For most tribes on the Great Plains, the pipe was the center of religious life. Because of its importance, it was often elaborately decorated with beadwork, as this Arapaho example illustrates. The cross in the center represents the four directions, another important symbol of their religion.

was hunting people in another part of the forest, dropped dead as the hunter thrust the stick into his heart.

After the hunter had struck the heart of the father, and so killed him, he then asked the dwarf in the tepee to whom the next heart belonged. The dwarf said that it belonged to his mother. After the dwarf had spoken the word, the hunter punched the heart with his sharp stick. The mother, who had been helping the father hunt for people in another part of the forest, dropped dead. The hunter then asked the dwarf in the tepee who were the owners of the different hearts and pierced each of them with the sharp stick, until he came to the last one at the door. "Whose heart is this, friend?" asked the hunter.

"Well, that is my own heart, friend," said the dwarf. The hunter pierced it, and the dwarf quickly died.

Thus these small cannibalistic people who left their hearts at home while they were out doing mischief were exterminated by the shrewd hunter.

STANDING THE WORLD ON ITS HEAD: STORIES OF THE TRICKSTER

The figure of the Trickster has always played a prominent role in the mythology of Native Americans, fascinating scholars as well as audiences. Paul Radin's *The Trickster: A Study in American Indian Mythology* created quite a stir upon its publication in 1956; it included essays written by such prominent academic figures as the anthropologist Stanley Diamond and the psychologist Carl Jung. One reason for this fascination is the fact that the Trickster has very few analogs in the mythologies of other cultures. To begin with, he is

This Tlingit ceremonial mask, made of wood and human hair, was worn by shamans and embodied the power of the Trickster, the fierce and cunning creator/destroyer god of many Native American tribes.

71

neither good nor bad. At times he seems benevolent, creating things and being generally humorous and delightful. At other times he is mischievous, even vicious, acting without regard to the impact his behavior has on either himself or others. To the scholar, such a mythic figure reveals the subtle thinking of a people, the values that they uphold, and the fears that they share.

To the Native American, Trickster represents nature, or more precisely the chaotic capacities of nature, which at times seems gentle and benevolent, at other times reckless and destructive. Trickster's personality is the personality of the weather, the water, and the wind—and is just as unpredictable.

In addition, Trickster illustrates the consequences of human beings acting in such a manner. It is this teaching aspect of Trickster tales that has puzzled so many readers. To the missionaries and ethnographers who first recorded these tales, the elements within

them seemed shocking: frequent references to sexual acts, many of them considered abnormal, even disgusting, by European standards. There are also many references to urination or defecation in these tales. Yet these are stories told not just to and by adults, but also to children, especially children specifically targeted as appropriate recipients of the story's "message." Of course, by European standards, many of these tales would not be considered suitable for children, but to the Native American, the scatological humor and the embarrassment generated by the sexual references made the stories particularly memorable. Children were told Trickster tales so that they could laugh, certainly, but also so that they might learn a valuable lesson in how not to behave toward each other. Trickster teaches brilliantly by negative example.

The tales themselves vary tremendously from tribe to tribe. Trickster is often associated with an animal, usually one considered tricky, or sneaky, by that particular tribe. Among the Lakota, he is called Spider Man (spiders were considered sly and untrustworthy by the Lakota); among most western tribes, he is associated with the coyote; and eastern tribes associated him with the blue jay, the raven, or the mink. In any case, he is a godlike figure, able to change his shape to suit his purpose, able to chop his body into bits and use the parts for his twisted aims, able to abuse people in any fashion imaginable, even if he often ends up abusing himself in the process.

This first tale comes from the Lakota tribe and has been retold in many versions, including one by Jenny Leading Cloud, recorded by Richard Erdoes in *American Indian Myths and Legends* (1984). It features Iktome (Lakota for Spider Man) and his friend Coyote—both of whom are seen as Tricksters, Coyote here presented as a sort of Trickster-in-training. In this tale Coyote learns a valuable lesson about gift-giving from the wise Iya.

This plains woman and her child dress ceremonially for the camera. She holds an Eagle feather fan and he has a warrior's medicine bag hanging from his belt.

COYOTE'S GIFT
TO IYA,
THE ROCK

[LAKOTA]

One day Coyote was walking along with his friend Iktome. Suddenly in their path stood a huge rock. This was not just any rock. It was a special rock with those spidery lines of green moss all over it, the kind that has power. It was Iya.

Coyote said, "Why, this is a nice-looking rock. I think it is important. I think it must be Iya." Coyote took off the thick blanket he was wearing and put it on the rock. "Here, Iya, take this as a present. Take this blanket, friend rock, to keep you from freezing. You must feel cold out here all alone."

"Wow, what a generous gift!" said Iktome. "You sure are in a giving mood today, friend."

"Ah, it's nothing. I'm always giving things away. Iya looks real nice in my blanket, don't you think?"

"I think it is his blanket now," said Iktome.

The two friends continued on down the path. Pretty soon a cold rain started to fall. The rain then turned to hail. The hail then turned to slush. Coyote and Iktome took refuge in a cave, but the cave was cold and wet. Iktome was pretty warm. He had his thick buffalo robe on. But Coyote had only his shirt, because he had given Iya his blanket, and he was shivering. In fact he was freezing. His teeth were chattering.

"My good friend," Coyote said to Iktome, "go back and get me my fine blanket. I need it, and that rock has no use for it. He's been getting along without a blanket for ages. Hurry, please, I'm freezing!"

Iktome went back to Iya, saying, "Can I have that blanket back, please?"

The rock said, "No, I like it. What is given is given."

Iktome returned and told Coyote, "He won't give it back."

"That no-good, ungrateful rock!" said Coyote. "Has he done anything to get the

blanket? Has he earned it? I'll go get it back myself."

"Friend," said Iktome, "Tunka, Iya, the rock—there's a lot of power there! Maybe you should just let him keep it."

"Are you crazy? This is an important blanket of many colors and great thickness, and I am cold. I'll go talk to him."

Coyote went back and told Iya, "Hey rock! What's the meaning of this? What do you need a blanket for? Let me have it back right now!"

"No," insisted the rock. "What is given is given."

"You're a bad rock! Don't you care that I'm freezing to death? That I'll catch a cold?" Coyote jerked the blanket away from Iya and put it on. "So there. That's the end of the argument."

"That is by no means the end of the argument," said the rock.

Coyote went back to the cave. The rain and hail soon stopped and the sun came out again, so Coyote and Iktome sat before the cave, sunning themselves, eating pemmican and fry-bread. After eating they took out their pipes and had a smoke.

All of a sudden Iktome said, "What's that noise?"

"What noise? I didn't hear anything."

"That rumbling noise, far off."

"Yes, friend, I think I hear it now."

"Friend Coyote, it's getting stronger and nearer, like thunder or an earthquake."

"It is getting rather strong and loud. I wonder what it can be."

"I have a pretty good idea, friend," said Iktome, looking scared.

Then they saw the great rock. It was Iya, rolling, thundering, crashing upon them.

"Let's run for it!" cried Iktome. "Iya means to kill us!"

The two ran as fast as they could as the rock rolled after them, coming ever closer.

"Friend, let's swim the river. The rock is so heavy, he surely can't swim!" cried Iktome. So they swam the river, but Iya, the great rock, also swam over the river as if he had been made of wood.

"Quickly, into the forest, among the big trees," cried Coyote. "That big rock surely can't get through this thick forest." Coyote and Iktome ran among the trees, but the huge Iya was unstoppable and came rolling after them, shivering and splintering the big pines to pieces, left and right.

The two came out onto the flat land. "Oh! Oh!" cried Iktome, very frightened indeed. "Friend Coyote, this is really not my quarrel. I just remembered, I have pressing business to attend to. So good-bye!" And, with that, Iktome ran away in another direction and left Coyote alone.

So Coyote ran on and on, with the big rock thundering close at his heels. Then Iya, the big rock, finally rolled right over Coyote, flattening him out altogether.

Iya took his blanket and rolled back to his own place, saying, "So there, that is the true end of the argument!"

Whenever Coyote is killed, he can make himself come to life again, but it took him the whole night to puff himself up into his usual shape. He was lucky someone didn't come along and make a rug out of him before he made it back to his normal size.

Friends, hear this advice: always be generous in heart. If you have something to give, give it forever.

•

This next tale comes from the Winnebago tribe. One version is included in Paul Radin's *The Trickster: A Study in American Indian Mythology* (1956). In this story, Trickster is outsmarted by a strange plant and his own headstrong nature.

The Lakota people, such as this warrior named Looking Elk, were particularly interested in Trickster stories. Even though their stories of Trickster were designed to teach children how not to behave, there is always a hint of begrudging admiration in each tale.

TRICKSTER
ARGUES WITH A
LAXATIVE BULB

[WINNEBAGO]

As he went wandering around aimlessly, Trickster suddenly heard someone speaking. He listened very carefully and the voice seemed to say, "He who chews me will defecate; he will be forced to defecate!" That was what the voice was saying. "Well, why is this person talking like this?" said Trickster. He then walked in the direction from which he had heard the voice, and again he heard, quite near him, someone saying, "He who chews me, he will have to defecate; he will be forced to defecate!" This is what was said. "Well, why does this person talk in such a rude fashion?" said Trickster. He continued walking along. Then right at his very side, a voice seemed to say, "He who chews me, he will have to defecate; he will be forced to defecate!" Trickster was perplexed.

"Well, I wonder who it is that is speaking. I know very well that if I chew it, whatever it is, I will not defecate." But he kept looking around for the speaker and finally discovered, much to his astonishment, that it was a bulb on a bush. It was the bulb who was speaking. So he seized it, put it in his mouth, chewed it, and then swallowed it. He did just this and then went on.

"Well, where is the bulb gone that talked so much? Why, indeed, should I defecate? When I feel like defecating, then I shall defecate, but no sooner. How could such an object make me defecate?!" said Trickster. Even as he spoke, however, he began to break wind. "Well, this, I suppose, is what it meant. Yet the bulb said I would defecate, and I am merely expelling gas. In any case, I am a great man

even if I do expel a little gas!" said Trickster. As he was talking, he again broke wind. This time it was really quite strong. "Well, what a foolish one I am. This is why I am called Foolish One, Trickster." Now he began to break wind again and again. "So this is why the bulb spoke as it did, I suppose." Once more he broke wind. This time it was very loud, and his rectum began to smart. "Well, it surely is a great thing!" Then he broke wind again, this time with so much force that he was propelled forward. "Well, well, it may even make me give another push, but it won't

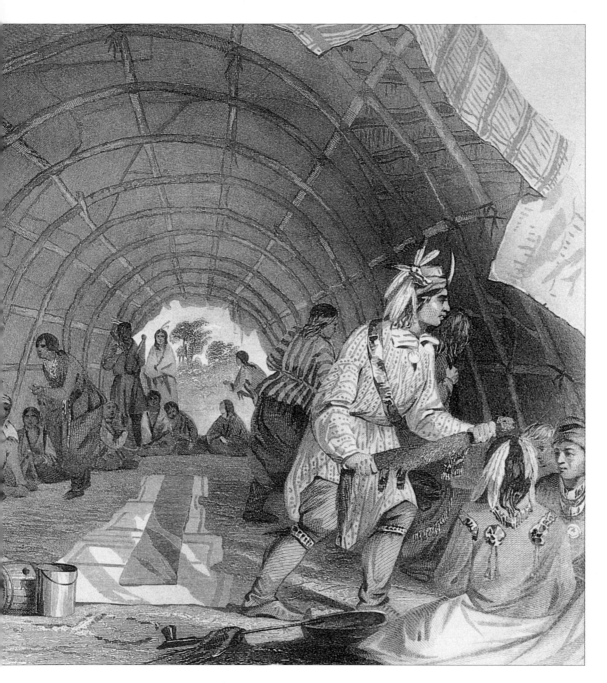

The Winnebago tribe of Wisconsin had such an elaborate cycle of Trickster tales that the anthropologist Paul Radin used their version when he transcribed them in the 1950s. In this scene, the Winnebago shamans prepare for a Medicine Dance.

make me defecate," he exclaimed defiantly. The next time he broke wind, the hind part of his body was raised up by the force of the explosion, and he landed on his knees and hands. "Well, go ahead and do it again! Go ahead and do it again!" Then he broke wind again. This time the force of the expulsion sent him far up in the air, and he landed on the ground, on his stomach. The next time he broke wind, he had to hang on to a log, so high was he thrown. After a while, he landed on the ground with the log landing on top of him. He was almost killed by the fall. The next

time he broke wind, he had to hold on to a tree that stood near by. It was a poplar, and he held on with all his might, yet nevertheless, even then, his feet flopped up in the air. Again he held on to it when he broke wind, and yet he pulled the tree up by the roots. He went on until he came to a large tree, a large oak tree. Around this he put both his arms. Yet when he broke wind, he was swung up and his toes struck against the tree. However, he was able to hold on.

Soon he proceeded onward. He seemed to have gotten over his troubles, for a time.

This George Catlin painting from the 1830s depicts Winnebago Indians shooting ducks in the early morning. Catlin lived among the tribe and painted them because of their "good-natured indulgence and handsome form."

"Well, this bulb did a lot of talking," he said to himself, "yet it could not make me defecate." But even as he spoke, he began to have the desire to defecate, just a very little. "Well, I suppose this is what it meant. It certainly bragged a good deal, however." As he spoke, he again had a desire to defecate. "Well, what a braggart it was! I suppose this is why it said this." As he spoke these last words, he began to defecate without being able to control it. He began to defecate a good deal. After a while, as he was sitting down, his body would touch the excrement. Thereupon he got on top of a log and sat down there, but even then he touched the excrement. Finally he climbed up a log that was leaning against a tree. However, his body still touched the excrement, so he went up higher. Even then he touched it, so he climbed still higher up. Higher and higher he had to go. He could not

stop defecating. Now he was on top of the tree. It was small and quite uncomfortable, but the excrement still grew.

Even on the very limb on which he was sitting he began to defecate. So he tried a different position. Because the limb, however, was very slippery, he fell right down into the excrement. Down he fell, down into the dung. In fact he disappeared in it, and it was only with very great difficulty that he was able to get out of it. His raccoon-skin blanket was covered with filth, and he came out dragging it after him. "I guess that bulb got the better of me after all," said Trickster.

•

In yet another tale, this one from the Tlingit tribe in the Pacific northwest, Trickster is shown to cause misfortune even when he sets out to be heroic. This tale, taken from several nineteenth- and twentieth-century sources, explains the origin of a common irritation.

HOW TRICKSTER CAUSED MOSQUITOES

[TLINGIT]

Long ago there was a giant who loved to kill humans, eat their flesh, and drink their blood. He was especially fond of human hearts. "Unless we can get rid of this giant," people said, "none of us will be left," and they called a council to discuss ways they could combat this giant.

Trickster came up about that time and said, "I think I know how to kill the monster," and he went to the place where the giant had last been seen. There he lay down and pretended to be dead.

Soon the giant came along. Seeing Trickster lying there, the giant said, "These Indians are making it easy for me. Now I don't even have to catch and kill them. They die right on my trail, probably from fear of me!"

The giant touched the body. "Ah, good," he said, "this one is still warm and fresh. What a tasty meal he'll make. I can't wait to roast his heart."

Like most north-western tribes, the Tlingit made highly elaborate basketry from various grasses woven and dyed, using a variety of roots, berries, and plants to produce the distinctive colors.

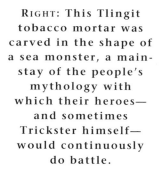

near the fireplace. Then he saw that there was no firewood and went out to get some.

As soon as the monster had left, Trickster got up and grabbed the giant's huge skinning knife. Just then the giant's son came in, bending low to enter. He was still small as giants go, and Trickster held the big knife to the boy's throat. "Quick tell me, where's your father's heart? Tell me or I'll slit your throat!"

The giant's son was scared. He said, "My father's heart is in his left heel."

Just then the giant's left foot appeared in the entrance, and Trickster swiftly plunged the knife into the heel. The monster screamed and fell down dead.

RIGHT: This Tlingit tobacco mortar was carved in the shape of a sea monster, a mainstay of the people's mythology with which their heroes—and sometimes Trickster himself—would continuously do battle.

BELOW: Two Tlingit girls, Tsacotna and Natsanitna, reveal the more Asiatic features of these northwestern people.

OPPOSITE, TOP: Made from wood, twine, copper, and animal skin, this shaman's helmet would have been used in specific ceremonies and rites of the Tlingit tribe.

OPPOSITE, BOTTOM: This Tlingit beaded bib displays the most prominant creature in northwestern mythology, the killer whale, a predator both admired and feared by these sea-going people.

Over his shoulder the giant flung Trickster, whose head hung down as if he were dead. Carrying Trickster home, the giant dropped him in the middle of the floor right

Despite being dead, the giant remained able to speak. "Though I'm dead, though you killed me, I'm going to keep on eating you—and all the other humans in the world—forever!"

"That's what you think!" said Trickster. "I'm about to make sure you never eat anyone again." He cut the giant's body into pieces and burned each one in the fire. Then he took the ashes and threw them into the air for the winds to scatter.

Instantly each of the particles turned into a mosquito. The cloud of ashes became a cloud of mosquitoes, and from their midst, Trickster heard the giant's voice laughing, saying, "Yes, I'll eat your people until the end of time."

And as the monster spoke, Trickster felt a sting, and a mosquito started sucking his blood, and then many mosquitoes stung him, and he began to scratch himself.

TWO WRAPPED IN ONE BLANKET: STORIES OF LOVE AND PASSION

Indian stories of love and passion often feature a Trickster character, though here the emphasis is more on humor than on a moral lesson or the foretelling of dire consequences. In these stories we find laughter and the lighter side of the Trickster dichotomy. Here Trickster is usually not destructive. Lustful perhaps, but no more so than any healthy young person, Trickster often gets himself into outrageous situations to satisfy the demands of his libido. Yet most of these tales have a happy ending, even for the Trickster himself.

The haunting expression of this Apache girl reminds us
of the inherent beauty of the Native American people.
Stories of great beauty and the love it inspires held
a special place among the legends these people told.

Another type of love tale, a type that doesn't involve Trickster, depicts the coming together of true lovers who have been separated because of circumstance. Often this joining requires the use of a love potion or some ceremony that induces love; therefore in these tales a shaman, or an animal who acts as a shaman, dominates the action by performing the ceremony or administering the potion.

In a third type of lusty tale, sacred clowns are depicted doing outrageous sexual acts meant to make the viewers and listeners laugh. For the Native Americans, laughter has great sacred power for healing, and sacred clowns, called *Heyokes* among the Lakota and *Koyemshi* (mudheads) among the Pueblos, are often part of serious, tribal ceremonies, which bring laughter and embarrassment to the participants at a time deemed appropriate by the holy men of the tribe.

This story was told by Henry Crow on the Rosebud reservation and recorded by Richard Erdoes. It tells the story of the flute, an instrument used among the plains tribes as part of the courting ritual.

HOW THE FLUTE CAME TO BE

[LAKOTA]

The *siyotanka* is for only one kind of music and that is love music. In the old days men would sit under a tree by themselves at night and make up their own special tunes, their own courting songs for their chosen *winchinchala*, their pretty young girl. The girl, lying on her buffalo robe, would listen to the courting song and would know, by the way it was played, which song belonged to her lover. If she chose, she could follow the sound and meet her lover under the tree. The flute is al-

ways made of cedarwood and is always in the shape of a bird with an open beak because of the legend that tells how flutes came to be.

Many generations ago, the people had drums, gourd rattles, turtle shell rattles, and bull roarers, but no flutes. A young man went out one day to hunt because his family was hungry. He found the tracks of an elk and he followed them, but he could never kill the elk. It always stayed just ahead of him. That night, he found himself deep in an unknown forest. He had lost the track of the elk, and he was lost. He lay down by a stream to get some rest and wait for morning, but he couldn't sleep because of the strange night sounds of the animals of the forest and the wind. Then he heard a new sound, a sound never before heard by anyone. It was strange and ghost-like and it made him afraid at first. But the sound was also like a song, a sad, mournful song, full of love, hope, and yearning. As he listened to the sound, he grew sleepy and finally drifted off. He began to dream of the woodpecker, *wagnuka*, who was singing the strange new song. Every so often, the woodpecker would stop and say: "Follow me and I will teach you."

This young girl, a member of the White Mountain Apache tribe, undergoes a puberty ritual after having covered herself with earth-paint.

the woodpecker for the gift, and returned to his village. Even though he had found no meat, he was happy.

But when he got home, the piece of cedar wouldn't make any noise at all and the young man was sad. He went to bed that night and dreamed of *wagnuka* again. The bird told him how to make a flute that worked. He watched the bird in his dream very carefully. When he woke, he went to a nearby forest and did exactly as he had seen the woodpecker do in his dream. He cut off a branch the right length, hollowed it out with a bow drill, carved the end to look like a bird's head, and painted it red. When he was finished, he fingered the holes the way the bird had in his dream and it produced the sound he heard in the forest the night before, the strange, ghost-like sound. The sound

When the young man awoke, he saw a real woodpecker on a nearby tree. The bird began to fly fron one tree to another and kept calling out "Come on!" to the young hunter. The hunter also began to once again hear the mournful sound he had heard the night before, and the bird was heading toward the sound. Finally it alit on a cedar tree and began to peck at it. There was a sudden gust of wind and the hunter heard the sound again, but this time he realized that it was coming from the dead branch the woodpecker sat on. He also realized that the sound was made by the wind as it went through the dead branch and the holes the woodpecker drilled. The young man broke off the branch, thanking

traveled to the village, and the people heard it and were astonished.

Meanwhile, there lived a big chief in the village who had a daughter who was very beautiful, but very proud. No young man was good enough for her. Many had come to court her, but she had sent all of them away. Now the young hunter had gotten it into his head that he wanted this girl for his own, but he never knew how to court her in a way she would appreciate. But now that he had made the flute, he decided to see if it wouldn't work a charm on her.

She was in her tepee when she heard the young man's music. At first, she did not want to go see who was making the beautiful music, but her feet wanted to go. She tried to stop them, but then her arms and head wanted to go, so she left the tepee and went outside and con-fronted the young man. "Young man," she said, "I am yours forever." She told him to get his father to send a gift to her father, and no matter how small the gift, it would be accepted.

And so the fathers quickly agreed to the wishes of their children, and the proud *winchinchala* became the young man's wife. All the other young men of the village had heard and seen how the young hunter had carved a flute and won the Chief's daughter, so they began to carve their own flutes. The practice spread from the tribe to tribe, making young girls' feet go where they shouldn't. And that is how the flute came to be among our people.

•

The following tale was recorded by Elsie Clews Parsons in 1940 and published by the American Folklore Society. It comes from the Pueblo tribe and concerns a jealous chief and his erring wife.

This nineteenth-century etching shows Pueblo shamans during a Clown Ceremony. They dressed in symbolic—often suggestive or ridiculous—costumes and would prance and frolic around, making people laugh at their often lewd antics in order to lift their spirits or heal their sorrow.

APACHE CHIEF PUNISHES HIS BRIDE

[PUEBLO]

The Apache people were traveling one day when they came upon a lake. They wanted to fetch water from the lake, but it was too shallow by the bank. They placed a large buffalo skull in the water to step on, thereby gaining access to the cleaner, deeper water. One day the chief's new bride, a pretty young woman, came to the lake to get water. She saw the skull and marveled. "What a handsome animal you were. I wish I could have seen you when you were alive."

At that, the skull became a big white buffalo, handsome and tall. "I am Big White Buffalo Chief," the animal said. The buffalo told her to get upon his head between his horns and he would take her with him to his people. She climbed up and they ran off.

When the Chief's wife did not return that evening, he went to look for her. He went to the lake, saw her forgotten basket, saw the skull was gone, and saw the buffalo tracks. He knew his wife had been taken by the buffalo spirit. He went back home and began to make spirit arrows. He made spirit arrows for many days, and when he had enough, he left his people and went in search of his bride.

Along the way he met Old Spider Woman, a sorceress of great power. She told him that his bride was now the bride of White Buffalo Chief, and that she was well protected. At night, the old woman claimed, she sleeps among the buffalo, with all of them standing around to protect her. Then she gave him some medicine to help him retrieve his wife.

When the Apache chief finally found the buffalo tribe, he crept up close and waited. That night, he blew the magic medicine the

Standing in front of their traditional "wickiup," these Apache children live in a culture rigid with customs and codes of conduct, especially regarding infidelity and the behavior of women.

old woman had given him toward the plain. The next morning the White Buffalo chief was furious and began to chase the Apache chief. He chased him across the plain into a strand of trees. The Apache chief and his bride climbed a tree and tried to hide, but the buffalo chief saw them and began to ram the tree. Just then, a crow flew into the tree and told the chief where to shoot his spirit arrows. With the crow's help, the Apache chief felled that mightly buffalo and killed him.

But then, as he was butchering the buffalo by the tree, the Apache chief's wife climbed down and stood beside him. She had tears in her eyes and tears running down her cheeks. When the Apache chief saw this, he was angry.

"Are you crying because I'm butchering this buffalo?"

"No, I'm crying because of the smoke."

But she continued to cry louder when he began butchering the animal again.

"You are crying because of this animal! After all this trouble, you still want him! Now you can die with him." And he took his bow and shot her with a spirit arrow and killed her. After that, he roamed the earth, looking for other women who choose to leave their husbands, seeking to do the same to them that he did to his own bride.

•

Based on a traditional Cherokee tale recorded in several sources, including James Mooney's *Myths of the Cherokee* (1902), this next tale explains the origin of the mole and his preference for being underground.

RIGHT: The Apache woman, along with all her other duties to the tribe, provided sole care of the children. This woman tends a small baby in a traditional Apache cradle basket.

OPPOSITE: Known for their tenacious stamina and courage, Apache warriors were among the most feared fighters on the southern plains.

OPPOSITE: Riding their ponies at full gallop, hunters shot the buffalo with arrows after singling out an individual from the herd. This technique, while dangerous and uncertain of success, was far more efficient than hunting the great beasts on foot as native people's ancestors had done.

LEFT: Native Americans viewed the mole not as a pest but as a creature with great power, able to "pop" up wherever or whenever from mother earth herself.

MOLE MAKES A LOVE MEDICINE

[CHEROKEE]

A young man was once in love with a young woman, but she disliked him and wanted nothing to do with him. He tried in every way to win her favor but with no success. At last he grew discouraged and made himself sick thinking about it.

Mole heard about this young man's misfortune and came to see him. Mole asked the young man to tell him the whole story. When he had finished, Mole said, "I can help you. I can make a love medicine that is very strong, even outdoing the so-called love medicines of your shamans. Not only will she like you, but she'll come to you of her own free will and right away."

The young man begged Mole to do this thing, so that night, burrowing underground to the place where the girl was in bed asleep, Mole took out her heart. Hearts are always used in love medicines. He came back with her heart and gave it to the discouraged lover, who was so full of despair and tears he couldn't see it even when it was in his hand. "There," said Mole, "swallow it, and she will be so drawn to you that she has to come."

The man swallowed the heart, and when the girl woke up, she somehow thought of the young man at once. She felt a strange desire to be with him, to go to him that minute. She couldn't understand it, because she had always really disliked him, but the feeling grew so strong that she was compelled to find the young man and tell him that she loved him and wanted to be his wife. And she did, and they were soon married.

All the shamans for miles around who heard of this love medicine were surprised and wondered how it had could have possibly come about. When they found out that it was the work of Mole, whom they had always thought too insignificant, too powerless to notice, they were immediately jealous and threatened to kill him. That's why even to this day Mole hides under the ground and still doesn't dare come up.

NOISES IN THE NIGHT: STORIES OF GHOSTS AND SPIRITS

Common to cultures around the world, stories about ghosts and spirits are probably the most universal category of mythology. Native American folklore includes a terrific variety of stories about the supernatural. Each tribe and tribal grouping had its own distinct beliefs concerning the afterlife, ranging from no belief at all to elaborate conceptions of the spirit world. Consequently, these stories are extremely varied, not lending themselves to many generalizations.

Like other tribes of the Northwest Coast, the Kwakiutl created elaborately carved and painted masks that were used in sacred rituals.

The Lakota had a belief that when death comes it is a mystery not to be solved or worried about, so the proper attitude would be to embrace it whenever it did arrive. This belief manifested itself in the often quoted phrase "It is a good day to die."

For the most part, Native American views of the hereafter are rather straightforward; the spirit world is pretty much like this one, and human spirits occupy themselves in much the same ways they did on earth, usually with all the weaknesses and limitations they had when they were alive. Ghosts and spirits are not usually considered wiser or more sacred, and they often dwell among the living. A man might suddenly discover his wife is a ghost, or perhaps that he himself is a ghost and has forgotten his death.

Unlike European stories and legends of ghosts, Native American tales are often hu-morous, though sometimes they have a more solemn and philosophical message. In either case the stories are meant to soothe people's fears about the afterlife, as well as to point out the warning that just because life ends it does not necessarily follow that your troubles will end as well. Often in these stories, the action will begin while the character is alive and con-tinue after his death.

This first tale is of the more humorous variety. It comes from the Lakota tribe and has been recorded in many sources, including an account by Ruth Benedict in "Serrano Tales," *Journal of American Folklore 39* (1926).

THE WARRIOR WITH NO FEAR

[LAKOTA]

Once there were four ghosts sitting together talking. One of them said, "I've heard of a young warrior who's afraid of nothing. He's not even afraid of us, they say."

The second ghost said, "I bet I could scare him."

The third ghost said, "We must try to make him so scared that he shivers and runs and hides."

The fourth ghost said, "Let's make a bet. Whoever can scare this warrior the most, wins." They agreed to bet their ghost horses.

Later this young warrior who was never afraid came walking along one night. The moon was shining, the stars were out. Sud-denly in his path the first ghost appeared, tak-ing the form of a skeleton. "Hou, friend," said the ghost, clicking his teeth together and making a sound like sticks clacking together.

"Hou, cousin," responded the young war-rior. "You're in my way. Get off the road and let me pass."

"Not until we have played the hoop-and-stick game. If you lose, I'll make you a skeleton like me."

The young man laughed. He took hold of the skeleton and bent it into a big hoop, tying it with some grass. He took one of the skeleton's leg bones for his game stick and rolled the skeleton along, scoring again and again with the leg bone. "Well, I guess I won this game," said the young warrior. "How about some shinny ball?"

The young warrior took the skeleton's skull and used the leg bone to drive it ahead of him like a ball.

"Ouch!" said the skull. "You're hurting me. You're giving me a headache."

"Well, you asked for it. Who proposed that we play this game, anyway, you or me? You sure are a silly ghost." The young warrior kicked the skull aside and walked on.

Farther on he met the second ghost, also in the form of a skeleton, who jumped at him with bony hands. "Let's dance, friend," the skeleton said.

"A very good idea, cousin ghost," said the young warrior. "What shall we use for a drum and drumstick? Oh, yes, I know!" Taking the ghost's thighbone and skull, the young warrior danced and sang, beating on the skull with the bone.

"Stop! Stop!" cried the skull. "This is no way to dance. You're hurting me. You're giving me a headache."

"You're lying, ghost," said the young warrior. "Ghosts can't get headaches."

"I don't know about other ghosts," said the skull, "but me, I'm hurting."

"For a ghost you're awfully sensitive," said the young warrior. "Really, I'm disappointed. There we were, having a good time, and you spoiled my fun with your whining. Go and groan somewhere else." The young warrior kicked the skull aside and scattered the rest of the bones all over.

"Now see what you've done," complained the ghost, "it will take me hours to get all my bones together. You're a very bad warrior."

"Stop your whining," said the young warrior. "It gives you something to do." Then he kept walking.

Soon he came upon the third ghost, another skeleton. "This is getting monotonous," said the young warrior. "Are you the same ghost as before? Did I meet you farther back?"

"No," said the ghost. "Those were my cousins. They're soft. But I'm tough. Let's wrestle. If I win, I'll make you into a skeleton like me."

"My friend," said the young warrior, "I don't feel like wrestling with you, I feel like

To the Lakota, bravery was a tangible thing, an attitude that would sustain a warrior as he faced challenges day to day. But being brave on the battlefield did not mean a warrior was never afraid, for there was always something which frightened every man, as illustrated in the story "The Warrior with No Fear."

sledding. There's enough snow on the hill for that. I should have buffalo ribs for it, but your rib cage will do."

The young warrior took the ghost's rib cage and used it as a sled. "This is fun!" he said, whizzing down the hill.

"Stop, stop," cried the ghost's skull. "You're breaking my ribs!"

The young warrior said: "Friend, you look funny without a rib cage. You've grown so short. Here!" And he threw the ribs into a stream.

"Look what you've done! What can I do without my ribs? I need them."

"Jump in the water and dive for them," said the young warrior. "You need a bath, and your woman will appreciate it."

"What do you mean? I am a woman!" said the ghost, insulted.

"With skeletons I can't tell, you pretty thing, you," he said, and he walked on.

Then he came upon the chief ghost, a skeleton riding a skeleton horse. "I've come to kill you," said the skeleton.

Trying to capture the dignity and stoic strength of the Lakota people, George Catlin painted this portrait of Little Bear, a Hunkpapa warrior.

The young warrior made faces at the ghost. He rolled his eyes. He showed his teeth and gnashed them. He made weird noises. "I'm a ghost myself, a much more terrible ghost than you are," he said.

The skeleton got scared and tried to turn his ghost horse, but the young warrior seized it by the bridle. "A horse is just what I want," he said. "I've walked enough. Get off!" He yanked the skeleton from its mount and broke it into pieces. The skeleton was whimpering, but the young warrior mounted the skeleton horse and rode it into camp.

Day was just breaking, and some women who were up early to get water saw him and screamed loudly. They ran away, and the whole village was awakened by their shrieking. The people looked out of their tepees and became frightened when they saw the young warrior on the ghost horse. As soon as the sun appeared, however, the skeleton vanished. Then the young warrior laughed.

The story of his ride on the skeleton horse was told all through the camp. Later he joined a group of men and started to brag about putting the four skeleton ghosts to flight. People shook their heads, saying, "This young warrior is really brave. Nothing frightens him. He is the bravest man in the world."

Just then a tiny spider was crawling up this young warrior's sleeve. When someone called his attention to it, he cried, "Eeeeech! Get this bug off me! Please, someone take it off, I can't stand spiders! Eeeeeeeeech!" He shivered, he writhed, and he carried on. A little girl laughed, stepped up to him, and took the spider off his sleeve.

•

This next story comes from the Kwakiutl tribe on the northwest coast and has been recorded in several places, including an account by the anthropologist Franz Boas in his *Kwakiutl Tales* (1936). The story confronts the problem of grief, and the origin of the song that makes grief bearable, the song traditionally sung by the Kwakiutl people when someone dies.

SPIRIT
COUNTRY

[KWAKIUTL]

The spirits live in four homes, each one deeper than the preceding one. Once a woman was crying on account of her dead father. They buried him, and she sat crying under the grave tree for four days. The people called to her, but she refused to leave. On the fourth day she heard somebody come who called her in this way: "I call you downward, Crying Woman."

Then she jumped up and the ghost voice said, "Follow me." The ghost then appeared to her and motioned for her to come. He went downward, and she followed him. They came to a house called Hemlock-Leaves-on-Back. They entered the house and an old woman was sitting near the fire. She said, "Ah, ah, ah, ah. Sit down near the fire." The ghosts then used poles to take down dry salmon, and prepared to roast it. They placed the cooked fish on a small food mat and broke it up and gave it to Crying Woman.

Just when she was about to take it, a person came in and invited her into another house called Maggots-on-Bark-on-Ground. Then the woman who lived in the first house said, "Ah, ah, ah, ah. Yes, go with her. They are higher in rank than we are." She followed the person who had invited her and entered the next house. She saw an old woman sitting by the fire who seemed to be the same one whom Crying Woman had seen first. And the old woman prepared the food in the same way, giving Crying Woman something to eat.

Just when she was about to eat, another woman came and invited her into her house, which was called Place-of-Mouth-Showing-on-the-Ground. The woman in the second house said, "Yes, go with her. They are higher

A woman mourns her dead lover, who lies above her in his natural tree funeral pyre. Customarily, the woman will mourn for as long as six weeks, moaning, slashing her arms with knives, and pulling out her hair in a ritual display of grief.

in rank than we are." When she entered, the same old woman seemed to be sitting by the fire. Again food was prepared for Crying Woman to eat.

When she was just about to begin, she was called by another person in the fourth house, called Place-of-Never-Return. Again the woman said, "They are higher in rank than we are, so go." When Crying Woman entered she saw her father sitting at the end of the house. And when he saw her he became angry and said, "Why do you come here? This is the place from which nobody ever returns. Whoever enters the first three houses may return. But if you come here, you must stay. Do not eat what is offered to you. Go back."

Then he called the ghosts to take her back.

When she returned, she was again lying under the grave tree, but was cold and motionless, like one dead. The ghosts came back singing the following song: "hama yahahaha, hama yahahaha, hama yahahaha, hama yahahaha." She was like one dead, but she came back. When her father had spoken to her, he had said, "When we take you back, we will sing so that the people may hear our song and sing it when others die."

Then they brought her up alive on a board. The people heard the song, but they did not see anyone. Then they took the board into the winter-dance house. This song they learned from Crying Woman, and it is now sung when others die.

•

This final tale comes from the Zuni tribe and has been taken from several nineteenth- and twentieth-century sources. It is a tale much like the story of Orpheus in Greek mythology, but here there is an added lesson concerning the inevitability of death that the warrior, in the end, must come to terms with before he can let his wife rest in peace.

THE
GHOST WIFE

[ZUNI]

A young man was once grieving because the beautiful young wife whom he loved was dead. As he sat at the graveside weeping, he decided to follow her to the land of the dead. He made many prayer sticks and sprinkled sacred corn pollen. He took a downy eagle plume and colored it with red earth color. He waited until nightfall, when the spirit of his departed wife came out of the grave and sat beside him. She was not sad, but smiling. The spirit maiden told her husband, "I am just leaving one life for another. So please do not weep for me."

"I cannot let you go," said the young man, "I love you so much that I will go with you to the land of the dead."

The ghost wife tried to dissuade him but could not overcome his determination. At last she gave in to his wishes, saying, "If you must follow me, know that I shall be invisible to you as long as the sun shines. You must tie this red eagle plume to my hair. It will be visible in daylight, and if you want to come with me, you must follow the plume."

The young husband tied the red plume to his ghost wife's hair, and at daybreak, as the sun slowly began to rise, the ghost wife started to fade from his view. The lighter it became, the more the form of his wife dissolved and grew transparent, until at last it vanished altogether. But the red plume did not disappear. It waved before the young man, a mere

This historical etching shows a young Zuni woman braiding the hair of another as she prepares for courtship, which was a system of elaborate ritual and custom among these southwestern people.

arm's-length away, and then, as if rising and falling on a dancer's head, it began leading the way out of the village, moving through the streets out into the fields, moving through a shallow stream, moving into foothills of the mountains, leading the young husband ever westward toward the land of the evening sun.

The red plume moved swiftly, evenly, floating without effort over the roughest trails, and soon the young man had trouble following it. He grew more and more tired and finally was totally exhausted as the plume left him farther behind. Then he called out, panting, "Beloved wife, wait for me. I can't walk any farther right now."

The red plume stopped, waiting for him to catch up, and when he did so, it hastened on. For many days the young man traveled, following the plume by day, resting during the nights, when his ghostly bride would sometimes appear to him, speaking encourag-

ing words. Most of the time, however, he was merely aware of her presence in some mysterious way. Day by day the trail they followed became rougher and rougher. The days were long, the nights short, and the young man grew more and more weary, until at last he had hardly enough strength to set one foot before the other.

One day the trail led to a deep, almost bottomless chasm, and as the husband came to its edge, the red plume began to float away from him into nothingness. He reached out to seize it, but the plume was already beyond his reach, floating straight across the canyon, because spirits can fly through the air.

The young man called across the chasm, "Dear wife of mine, I love you. Wait for me!"

He tried to descend one side of the canyon, hoping to climb up the opposite side, but the rock walls were sheer, with nothing to hold onto. Soon he found himself on a ledge

These young Zuni tribesmen display the traditional dancers' costumes at the famed Gallup Intertribal Ceremonial Dance held in New Mexico.

barely wider than a thumb, from which he could go neither forward nor backward. It seemed that he must fall into the abyss and be dashed into pieces. His foot had already begun to slip, when a tiny striped squirrel scooted up the cliff, chattering to him, "You young fool, do you think you have the wings of a bird or the feet of a ghost? Hold on for just a little while and I'll help you." The little creature reached into its cheek pouch and brought out a little seed, which it moistened with saliva and stuck into a crack in the wall. With his tiny feet, he danced above the crack, singing, "Tsithl, tsithl, tsithl, tall stalk, tall stalk, tall stalk, sprout, sprout quickly." Out of the crack sprouted a long, slender stalk, growing quickly in length and breadth, sprouting

leaves and tendrils, spanning the chasm so that the young man could cross over without any trouble.

On the other side of the canyon, the young man found the red plume waiting, dancing before him as ever. Again he followed it at a pace so fast it seemed that his heart would burst from the strain. At last the plume led him to a large, deep, dark lake, and the plume plunged into the water to disappear below the surface. Then the husband knew that the land of the dead lay at the bottom of the lake. He was in despair because he could not follow the plume into the deep. In vain did he call for his ghost wife to come back. The surface of the lake remained undisturbed and unruffled like a sheet of mica. Not even at

The Zuni people often prayed to their ancestors at decorated altars commemorating the dead.

The Zuni landscape is as forbidding as the people's myths of the afterlife, as this scene of a Zuni cornfield near Corn Mesa attests.

nighttime did his ghost wife reappear. The lake, the land of the dead, had swallowed her up. As the sun rose above the mountains, the young man buried his face in his hands and wept.

Then he heard someone gently calling, "Hu-hu-hu," and he felt the soft beating of wings on his back and shoulders. He looked up and saw an owl hovering above him. The owl said, "Young man, why are you weeping?"

He pointed to the lake, saying, "My beloved wife is down there in the land of the dead, where I cannot follow her."

"I know, poor man," said the owl. "Follow me to my house in the mountains, where I will tell you what to do. If you follow my advice, all will be well and you will be reunited with the one you love."

The owl led the husband to a cave in the mountains, and as they entered, the young man found himself in a large room full of owl men and owl women. The owls greeted him warmly, inviting him to sit down and rest, to eat and drink. Gratefully he took his seat.

The old owl who had brought him took his owl clothing off, hanging it on an antler jutting out form the wall, and revealed him-

self as a manlike spirit. From a bundle in the wall, this mysterious being took a small bag, showing it to the young man, telling him, "I will give this to you, but first I must instruct you in what you must do and must not do."

The young man eagerly stretched out his hand to grasp the medicine bag, but the owl man drew back. "Foolish fellow, you suffer from the impatience of youth! If you cannot curb your eagerness and your youthful desires, then even this medicine will be of no help to you."

"I promise to be patient," responded the husband.

"Well, then," said the owl man, "this is sleep medicine. It will make you fall into a deep sleep and transport you to some other place. When you awake, you will walk toward the morning star. Following the trail to the middle anthill, you will find your ghost wife there. As the sun rises, so she will rise and smile at you, rise in the flesh, a spirit no more, and so you will live happily.

"But remember to be patient. Remember to curb your eagerness. Let not your desire to touch and embrace her get the better of you, for if you touch her before bringing her safely home to the village of your birth, she will be lost to you forever."

Having finished this speech, the old owl man blew some of the medicine on the young husband's face, who instantly fell into a deep sleep. Then all the strange owl men put on their owl coats and, lifting the sleeper, flew with him to a place at the beginning of the trail to the middle anthill. There they laid him down underneath some trees.

Then the strange owl beings flew on to the big lake at the bottom of which the land of the dead was located. The old owl man's magic sleep medicine and the feathered prayer sticks that the young man had carved enabled them to dive down to the bottom of

Decorated pottery such as this Zuni kiva bowl would serve shamans inside the ringed structure where most Zuni ceremonies took place.

the lake and enter the land of the dead. Once inside they used the sleep medicine to put to sleep the spirits who are in charge of that strange land beneath the waters. The owl beings reverently laid their feathered prayer sticks before the altar of that netherworld, took up the beautiful young ghost wife, and lifted her gently to the surface of the lake. Then taking her upon their wings, they flew with her to the place where the young husband was sleeping.

When the husband awoke, he saw first the morning star, the middle anthill, and then his wife at his side, still in slumber. Then she too awoke and opened her eyes wide, at first not knowing where she was or what had happened to her. When she discovered her lover right by her side, she smiled at him, saying, "Truly, your love for me is strong, stronger than love has ever been, otherwise we would not be here."

They got up and began to walk toward the pueblo of their birth. The young man did not forget the advice the old owl man had given him, especially the warning to be patient and shun all desire until they had safely arrived at their home. In that way they traveled for four days, and all was well.

On the fourth day, they arrived at Thunder Mountain and came to the river that flows by Salt Town. Then the young wife said, "My husband, I am very tired. Let me rest here awhile, and then, refreshed, we can walk the last short distance home together." And her husband said, "We will do as you say."

The wife lay down and fell asleep. As her lover was watching over her, gazing at her loveliness, desire so strong he could not resist it overcame him, and he stretched out his hand and touched her.

She awoke instantly with a start, and, looking at him and at his hand upon her body, began to weep, the tears streaming down her face. At last she said, "You loved me,

but you did not love me enough. Otherwise you would have waited. Now I shall die again." And before his eyes her form faded and became transparent, and at the place where she had rested a few moments before, there was nothing. On a branch of a tree above him, the old owl man hooted mournfully, "Shame, shame, shame." Then the young man sank down in despair, burying his face in his hands, and ever after his mind wandered as his eyes stared vacantly.

If the young lover had controlled his desire, if he had not longed to embrace his beautiful wife, if he had practiced patience and self-denial for only a short time, then death would have been overcome.

But then if there were no death, people would crowd each other because there would be more people on this earth than the earth can hold. Then there would be hunger and war, with people fighting over every tiny patch of earth, over every ear of corn, and over every scrap of meat. So maybe what happened was for the best after all.

This Zuni frog and butterfly pot held special meaning in a culture steeped in myth and tradition.

BIBLIOGRAPHY

Benedict, Ruth. "Serrano Tales." *Journal of American Folklore 39* (1926): 8.

———. *Zuni Mythology*. Columbia University Contributions to Anthropology, volume 21. New York: Columbia University Press, 1935.

Bierhorst, John. *The Red Swan: Myths and Tales of the American Indians*. New York: Farrar, Straus, and Giroux, 1976.

Boas, Franz. *Kwakiutl Tales: New Series*. Columbia University Contributions to Anthropology, volume 26, parts 1 and 2. New York: Columbia University Press, 1936.

———. *Tsimshian Mythology*. Bureau of American Ethnology Annual Report No. 31. Washington, D.C.: United States Government Printing Office, 1916.

Curtis, Natalie. "Creation Myths of the Cochans (Yuma Indians)." *The Craftsman 16* (1909): 559–567.

Dorsey, George, and Alfred Kroeber. *Traditions of the Arapaho*. Chicago: Field Columbian Museum Publication 81, Anthropological Series, Volume 5, 1903.

Erdoes, Richard, and Alfonzo Ortiz. *American Indian Myths and Legends*. New York: Pantheon Books, 1984.

Forde, Daryll. *Folk-lore*, volume 41. London: William Glaisher for the Folk-lore Society, 1930.

Hobson, Geary. *The Remembered Earth: An Anthology of Contemporary Native American Literature*. Albuquerque, N.Mex.: University of New Mexico Press, 1979.

Kroeber, Alfred. "Cheyenne Tales." *Journal of American Folklore 13* (1900): 161–191.

Lame Deer, John (Fire), and Richard Erdoes. *Lame Deer: Seeker of Visions*. New York: Washington Square Press, 1972.

Momaday, N. Scott. "Man Made of Words." *The Remembered Earth: An Anthology of Contemporary Native American Literature*. Albuquerque, N.Mex.: University of New Mexico Press, 1979.

Mooney, James. *Myths of the Cherokee*. Bureau of American Ethnology Annual Report No. 19. Washington: United States Government Printing Office, 1902.

Nicolar, Joseph. *The Life and Traditions of the Red Man*. Bangor, Maine: C.H. Glass, 1893.

Radin, Paul. *The Trickster: A Study in American Indian Mythology*. New York: Schocken Books, 1956.

Starr, Jean. *Tales from the Cherokee Hills*. Winston-Salem, N.C.: John Blair Publishing, 1988.

Turner, Frederick W. *The Portable North American Indian Reader*. New York: Penguin Books, 1974.

Wood, Charles, and Scott Erskine. *A Book of Tales: Being Some Myths of the North American Indians*. New York: Vanguard Press, 1929.